A HUNDRED TO ONE

Pat Sheedy was born and raised in Limerick. He is a sports fanatic who completed a creative writing degree while in prison for crimes connected to his gambling addiction. He has won the short-story prize at the Listowel Writers' Week two years in a row.

A HUNDRED TO ONE

100 CONVICTIONS
1 MILLION EURO
THE DEVASTATING TRUE STORY
OF A COMPULSIVE GAMBLER

PAT SHEEDY

GILL BOOKS

Gill Books
Hume Avenue
Park West
Dublin 12
www.gillbooks.ie

Gill Books is an imprint of M.H. Gill and Co.

9781804580585

Designed by Typo•glyphix, Burton-on-Trent
Edited by Sylvia Tombesi-Walton
Proofread by Emma Dunne
Printed and Bound in the UK using 100% Renewable Electricity at CPI Group (UK) Ltd
This book is typeset in 11/18 pt Minion Pro.

The paper used in this book comes from the wood pulp of sustainably managed forests.

A CIP catalogue record for this book is available from the British Library.

5 4 3 2 1

MIX
Paper | Supporting
responsible forestry
FSC® C171272

To the late Paul O'Rourke, who always inspired me
and improved the lives of countless others.

To anyone and everyone
affected by gambling addiction.

'Every new beginning comes
from some other beginning's end ...'

PROLOGUE

t's a dirty, foggy, misty morning. My stomach has been churning since yesterday. All sorts of thoughts are going through my head.

Is Mam going to be okay?

Have I got everything I need in my bag?

What are my sisters going to think?

What are the lads going to say?

I'm sitting outside the courthouse. I need to be called, as there are entry restrictions due to COVID-19. I'm freezing and getting soaked, but I'm oblivious to it all. I'm in another world mentally – and about to enter another one physically.

The text beep sounds. I take my phone from my pocket. It's from Denise, my solicitor. 'Come now … Court 3,' it says. I take a deep breath, grab my bag and head for the door.

When I get into Court 3, I'm relieved that there's nobody there except the prosecution barristers and my legal team. I then notice the arresting gardaí in the corner. I take my place in the area reserved for the defendants. My goose, 36 years in the making, is finally cooked.

Judge Tom O'Donnell arrives, takes his seat and gets straight to the point. He's a decent man, and I am hoping for the best but not really expecting it.

'In the matters of sheets 84 and 85, I sentence you to three years.

However, due to the delay in sentencing, which was in no way your fault, I reduce this to two years.'

My heart sinks at the initial sentence but lifts a bit when he announces the reduction. I take great heart from this. Two years, less remission, leaves me with 18 months. With good behaviour, I can get that reduced further. *This isn't so bad*, I think to myself.

'In the matter of Sheet 87, I sentence you to 12 months,' the judge then says. The next words he speaks are crucial.

'To be served consecutively.'

My heart sinks again. Consecutive sentencing means that the sentence handed down will be added to the sentence already given. The word I wanted, needed, to hear was concurrent. That way it would be served within the initial two-year sentence. So now I am sentenced to three years. The 'not so bad' sentiment has totally vanished. I thought I would take the news badly. I envisaged fainting, crying, pleading. Instead, I just sit there, in acceptance. And I don't know why. My initial reaction to all previous times I thought I was going to be imprisoned was immediate panic, fear and trepidation. This time, there is an eerie acceptance of my fate. I don't know why I am as calm as I am. I tell myself it is me finally accepting things: I am finally going to end up where I deserve to be. The towel is thrown in, the white flag furiously waving.

I give instructions to my solicitor about contacting my family. I grab my bag and walk towards the holding cells, accompanied by a prison officer.

Finally, it is here. The fruits of my being a hopelessly compulsive gambler. It finally dawns upon me that I'm not as clever as I thought I was, and that those consequences I have been warned about for so many years are finally here.

My new life is just beginning.

CHAPTER 1

'm writing this as a gambling addict. What I write here are my recollections and experiences that have led me to where I am today. I've read lots of biographies and autobiographies over the years. Most of them include a chapter or two to describe childhood years and the early experiences that made you what you are today. A lot of these chapters tell of neglect, abuse and bad influences that helped shape the lives of whoever the story is about. I'm going to keep that brief for a few reasons, my family being the main one. I've embarrassed them enough over the years as it is.

I had a normal upbringing. I was reared by a mother and father who had many faults, but many, many more good points. We never had an abundance of anything, but we never went hungry, unwashed, cold or scruffy a day in our lives. I have two sisters – Lisa, who is two years older than me, and Niamh, who is seven years younger. Both are remarkable women who have reared their own families and carved out very successful careers.

I was never misled or encouraged by anyone to do the things I've done. I've always operated solo, in my own Walter Mitty-type world. I did so because that's how I liked it – secretive and personal, which allowed me to justify to myself that I wasn't actually harming anybody but myself. One of the many lies I fed myself as I continued to spiral out of control.

I've had self-esteem issues for as long as I can remember. In primary school, I was constantly teased for having bright red hair, a face full of freckles and big reading glasses. I went to a local school where I had no problem making friends, but I was also the target of some of the bullies. I endured this all the way through primary school. I was smarter than most in all of my classes. This also made me a target. Thankfully, the only time it ever got physical was in the classroom, usually at the hands of a frustrated Christian Brother who was very obliging when it came to either a flurry of fists or his thick, black leather strap. I didn't take it personally because it wasn't personal – several other lads in the class took the same punishment or worse.

In 1981 the time came for me to go to secondary school. There was a new comprehensive school just a stone's throw from the estate we lived in. But my mother wanted better for me, and she fought hard to get me into a school that at the time was considered to be among the best in Limerick City, and it still is. This school was the polar opposite of the primary school I had come from. For starters, there was a uniform to be worn, with a tie.

Then there were the students. These guys didn't have the raw, earthy, lingering Limerick Citaaaaay accent that all the lads in primary had. They spoke eloquently, slowly, many of them showing off the braces Mommy and Daddy had just spent more on than my father probably earned in a month. There was even a lad called Karl in my class. Karl? What kind of name was that? To me, Karl was a girl's name.

I quickly learned that this wasn't going to be the academic picnic primary school had been. I had gone from being top of the class to being bang average. I wasn't being slagged about the ginger hair or glasses anymore, either. In fact, I was almost ignored, except for the few friends who had also come along from primary school. And I didn't like that. I now realise and understand that this was the beginning of my lifelong quest to be popular. I walked through the school gates for the first time, and I immediately started drifting into another world. My own Walter Mitty world.

Finally, I found a way to get noticed. The posh boys didn't like to get dirty, literally. I went from being mediocre at sports in primary school to being the best at it in secondary. This was in no way down to my ability, but rather the fact that the majority of the posh boys were absolutely useless. I captained the rugby team, and I also boxed competitively with a fair degree of success. Suddenly, I was in demand … the posh boys wanted tips and hints from me, and they came to me in the yard, rather than me chasing friends. This boosted my ego to no end, and the Walter Mitty in me was truly established. After school and at weekends, I was back home, with my real friends, playing 'three goals in' and rounders. Back to the reality of mediocrity. I couldn't wait for school.

Looking back, I was envious of the posh boys. They lived in big detached houses and got dropped off at school by Daddy in his Mercedes. I walked to and from school, thankful in many ways that the posh boys wouldn't have to see my father's 10-year-old Hillman Hunter. I remember one day we were playing a school from across town in a rugby game. All my life I had wanted Dad to come and watch me play any kind of match, and to my surprise, he volunteered to be one of the designated drivers for the day. I was thrilled. The thrill quickly turned to embarrassment, however, when I overheard one or two of the other lads taking the mickey out of the 'state of the banger' we were being brought to the game in.

I was embarrassed to come from a council estate. I'm ashamed to admit that today. Looking back, there's no other place I'd want to have grown up in. Those were the times that I developed massive insecurity, fear and a desire for a materialistic life. They were also the times that I began to develop a web of lies, to become deceitful and subconsciously make the decision that I was going to do things that kept me at the top of the popularity tree. Life was about to get very colourful – and dangerous.

CHAPTER 2

I was a very young boy on the first occasion I set foot in a betting shop. I was 12 years old. I remember this because I had just made my confirmation. My father – who would never be anything but a social gambler – was hungover, and he asked me to run down to Bambury Bookmakers in Thomondgate, close to where we lived, to back three horses for him. I think the total cost of the bet came to 30p … hardly likely to put a hole in the weekly budget, but enough to give him an interest in the afternoon's racing on TV.

I ran down, dreaming in my head about how many goals Frank Stapleton might score for United later, about how Shannon RFC would fare in their afternoon game against whoever they were playing, where I would be a ball boy, and how Limerick United would do tomorrow at Markets Field. I was a sports-mad kid, only average at best at whatever I played. But I played them all: soccer, rugby, hurling, Gaelic football … and I loved the little dream world in which I existed. It helped me escape – from what, I didn't know at the time, but I do now.

When I got to the bookies, it was a small, poky room covered in a haze of cigarette smoke and populated by what I considered old men … guys in their mid-20s up to their 70s. I got several affectionate pats on the head from them, and I remember waiting a while, taking in all that was going on around me. There were all walks of life in there. Quiet guys trying to study form from the newspapers stuck to the walls, guys talking about what was going on in the world, guys pissing and moaning about what they had married, how much they had drunk last night or how much they were going to drink tonight. And not one of them slagged me about having red hair, freckles and glasses. Not one of them slagged me about what I was wearing, or about me constantly trying to impress the teachers at school.

'I could get to like this environment,' I thought.

I placed my father's bet. The kind lady behind the counter wrote it out for me on a betting slip. That's when I pulled off my first-ever scam. I thought it was ingenious. Just like several of the scams that I would create over the next 40 years: well thought out and well carried out, but stupid to their core and so easy to get caught out on.

Back then, when a bet was placed, it was written on a slip and duplicated on the page beneath by a sheet of carbon paper. The cashier stamped the bet and gave you the counterfoil as proof of your bet. No computers to capture your bet, no technology. I figured if I placed the bet for 10p, I could alter the amount written on the docket from 10p to 30p, pocket the difference and nobody would be any the wiser. After all, I could remember my dad muttering to himself that he never won, that you could never trust those bloody jockeys. Easy money for me – or so I thought, and 20p in my pocket in 1981 was four weeks' worth of pocket money. Then came the problem.

The three horses won, and I had placed the bet for only one-third of its value. I'm not going to pretend to remember how much Dad won off the bet. It might have been a tenner, which was a nice wedge back then, considering it was 40p a pint and less than £1 for a packet of the Gold Bond cigarettes my mother loved. But when he went in to collect, he was shocked to be given only a third of his winnings, and he was shown the original slip I submitted. I knew there was something wrong when I heard the front door slam. That was the first clue. The second clue was the shouts of 'Where is the little bastard?' The third and final clue came with the well-deserved wallop or two that followed.

This was the first of many clashes I had with my parents over the next few years. None too serious, and probably none that raised too many flags that would have indicated to them what I would become or how my life – and, as a result, their lives – would pan out.

It's 7.45 a.m. I can hear John the Man's radio show blaring downstairs. That's my alarm call. I get up and go straight downstairs, not even bothering to try and get into the bathroom. After all, I have a 16-year-old sister, two years older than I am, and she's got a boyfriend who goes to the school across the road from hers. She's not to be messed with, and she's doing whatever 16-year-old girls do to look good for their boyfriends.

I can smell the smoke emanating from Mam's third Gold Bond of the morning. Christ, I really hate cigarette smoke. It totally puts me off my cornflakes. My kid sister (seven years younger) won't eat her breakfast until she hears John the Man boom out over the airwaves that any child who doesn't eat their breakfast won't get anything from Santa … the Weetabix soon disappear, and she's ready for school.

My mate Martin calls at 8.35. He's as predictable as the Angelus. I know when I have to have my cornflakes finished by and to be ready. We know that it's exactly an 18-minute walk to school from my house. School starts at 9 a.m., and it's usually up to Mac's shop at lunchtime. Large groups of boys on one side of the car park, the girls from Salesians on the other. A chance for some courting couples to hold hands.

I've decided today that I'm not going back to school in the afternoon. A friend of mine who lives around the corner is in the process of opening a new gym in town. There's a lot of work to be done to it, and he's promised me a part-time job when it opens. Double geography with Beaker or getting paid a tenner for helping set things up in the new gym? A total no-brainer. Beaker can go bore the shite out of the rest of the lads … it's not for me.

In the gym, all the guys are older than me. I've discarded the school uniform and put on a tracksuit to fit in and not look like a schoolboy. God, I hate being a kid. I want to be grown up like these guys. Be able to understand their jokes and innuendos. I work for three hours, then quickly change back into my school uniform so Mam doesn't know I've gone on the hop. I'm happy as a pig in shit, though: I got to spend the afternoon with cool guys and earned a tenner in the process.

The next morning, I get up with a pep in my step. It's Saturday. No school tie to knot, no school bag to pack. No cigarette smoke blown into my face at breakfast. No battle for the bathroom. Everyone in my house loves a lie-in on a Saturday, except me. I'm up, already downstairs rifling through my father's pockets to see what change I'll find. Saturday mornings are always productive for me. On Friday nights, after a few pints, he always throws a few quid in loose change into his coat pocket – I know he won't remember.

In the early afternoon, I decide to go for a stroll earlier than usual. I normally head up to Thomond Park and watch a rugby match. They always kick off at 2.30 p.m. So, today at 1 p.m. I set off, down by Hassett's Cross. If I continue straight, I head towards town via the park and my school. But I turn left. Deliberately. By turning left, I am walking up towards Bambury's … the same bookies where I felt so accepted the last time I was there. I get to the door and peek in. Today it's really busy, being a Saturday. I say hello to a few of the men, most of whom grunt a curt reply. Up by the area where the board marker stands (that's the guy who writes the current prices of the horses in each race), I see a guy I know because he calls weekly to our house to collect for a rugby club lotto. We get talking, and he asks me if I fancy anything. I pretend to know what I'm talking about and start reading the form page on the wall. I look at the next few races and write out the names of four horses – partly because I like the sound of their names, and partly because the guy in the paper thinks they are going to win. I eagerly watch what's going on at the counter, what kind of bets are being placed and how much on average these guys are betting. I place two bets, each for a pound. Both lose … one by a mile, the other by inches. But it feels good.

I still have the slip with the four horses written out on it, so I go and ask the man I know what type of bet I can do. He looks at the four horses and kind of smirks. He suggests a Yankee. This is a type of bet where you won't lose if two of your horses win, you'll turn a profit if three do, and win a nice amount should all four win. I would like to do this, but you have to multiply your stake by 11 to include all bets. This sounds rather complicated to me, so I go with another option called an accumulator. This type of bet is exactly as it sounds: four horses picked. If the first one wins, your winnings roll over to the second, then the third and, if you're lucky, the fourth. I place a 50p accumulator on my four horses and retreat to the corner where I can hear the race commentaries.

One hour later, three of my horses have run and – amazingly – won. Word has started to filter around the shop that the ginger kid in the tracksuit has a 'decent accum going' and is waiting on the last horse.

'Well, kid … best of luck.'

'Hope ta' fuck he comes in for you.'

'About time someone took money off dem bastards.'

These are the comments I hear every minute.

The race goes off. I'm trying very hard to hear the commentary. By now, there's a crowd gathered around me; guys I don't know from Adam patting me on the shoulder, wishing me good luck. I'm totally caught up in the moment, I can't hear or see a thing due to shouting and cigarette smoke, but the next thing I know, I'm being hoisted up in the air and shaken with some vigour. My final horse has just come in.

There are no fancy computers here settling and capturing bets. It's all done manually, and telephone calls have to be made to the head office to verify everything. About 20 minutes later, all the to and fro is complete, and I go up to collect my winnings. I'm expecting another tenner or so to match the one I earned yesterday. Happy days. Not many young fellas my age have 20 quid to their name, including the posh boys at school. The overworked, red-faced lady behind the counter calls me, takes my docket and hands me £51. My bet was a near 100/1 shot. I can't feel my legs.

Fifty-one pounds. Dear, sweet Jesus!

On my way home, my head is racing. How and where am I going to hide this money? I'm also looking over my shoulder because a well-known bully and thief was in the bookies, and he might be following me home. I really should give Mam and Dad a fair chunk of this. They need it. But then I'd have to explain where I got it, and that wouldn't end well. I'll just have to hide it, but that's a problem for later. I'm heading into the shop now, and buying myself the most expensive ice pop and drink they have.

I'm just home. Dad asks me how Shannon got on. And then it hits me: I have missed the rugby match because I was in the bookies and lost track of time. I don't even know the score of the United game. I make up some bullshit about having to go into school for a few hours for a project and missing the game as a result.

The lying, scheming and manipulating had well and truly started. So had the secrecy and deceit. And I slowly but surely started to retreat into Walter Mitty land.

CHAPTER 3

Growing up in the mid-1980s was every bit as great as they say it was. I met my first true love when I was 16, as you do. We met every day walking to and from school and spent Saturdays together with friends. I was part of a clique and felt cool as ice. I was very popular, involved in sports and doing well in school. We went to big concerts and gigs like U2, Simple Minds, The Smiths, Big Country and others. Life was pretty good. And there was little or no gambling other than the Grand National.

My girlfriend outgrew me when I was 17. She was a year older and off to college to become a nurse. We broke up – I don't think it was cool for a college student to be dating a 'boy' who was still in secondary school. I took it pretty badly. It was the first time my heart was broken. It wouldn't be the last.

Naturally, the clique started to split, as most were off to college in different parts of the country. My best friend went off to Dublin to join the Civil Service. All of a sudden, I was alone – or at least, I felt like I was. In reality, I still had plenty of friends, both at home and at school, but somehow this wasn't enough. They weren't mature enough for me, and I found it very hard to be stimulated by any kind of interaction with them. So, after my Leaving Cert the following year, I started to make changes. Changes that would mould and determine my future.

I decided that in order to ingratiate myself with the type of people I wanted to move and shake with, I needed money. I saw an advert for a summer job selling advertising space for a weekly property newspaper. I went in, met the owner, and he decided to give me a go. Other than an outgoing personality and an ability to talk shite, I had no real experience. However, it turns out that to be a successful advertising salesperson, the most important attributes are an outgoing personality and an ability to talk shite!

I worked hard. I was on a commission basis, and I was making around £60–£80 a week, which was damn good for a 17-year-old kid. I became friendly with one of the more experienced sales reps, a guy called Eamon (who was older than me). Eamon was a good guy: we'd go for the odd pint or two after work, and I enjoyed working with him.

One day, Eamon asked me to meet him in the pub around the corner for a bowl of soup but to tell nobody we were meeting. Something was wrong, I thought, and I couldn't wait for lunchtime to come so I could find out what was going on. When I got there, Eamon was seated with a big, imposing man who introduced himself as Jim. Jim was full of life, very flamboyant and exuberant. I was immediately drawn to him. It turns out that Jim was launching a new newspaper, one that specifically focused on sports and social activities. And he wanted Eamon and me to work in the advertising department. I don't think I ever felt so important in my whole life. The pay was better, the offices fancier. It was a no-brainer.

We started work there the following week, and it turned out to be everything I wanted. Because it was a sports and social newspaper, we were invited to everything: matches, openings, bars and nightclubs, and we were treated like royalty wherever we went. And I was getting paid for it. Every day on the way home, I'd pass my first true love's house. For a long time after she so cruelly dumped me and broke my heart, I had felt like bursting into tears when I did this, but now I was bursting with pride, often muttering to myself, *Look at me now ... see what I've become.*

I wasn't doing a whole lot of gambling at this time, either. I guess this was because my self-esteem issues were apparently resolved due to my job and social standing. Then, one Monday morning, the giant bubble in which I was living burst.

Eamon and I went to work as usual. But this time it was different. When we got to the office, there was nothing there. No computers, no desks, no phones, no pictures on the wall. Even the kettle and toaster were gone. There were no letters, no clues ... nothing! This was a time when there were no mobile phones. We checked the pub across the road where Jim spent a lot of time drinking coffee ... no sign of him. We went to his house ... no answer. No car. Curtains drawn. We simply didn't know what to do. We went back to the pub in the hope that Jim would arrive and tell us what was going on. Perhaps, we speculated, he's moving us to a bigger office because things are going so well? Deep down, we both had a pretty good idea of what had happened. Jim had taken out a huge loan, never paid any bills for the nine months we had been in business, got prepaid for a lot of advertising and jumped on a plane to the USA with his wife and kids. Never to be seen again. And owing Eamon and me a few hundred quid in commission. We'd been screwed. I was devastated, and not just about the money. The lifestyle to which I had become accustomed was now in huge jeopardy. This both scared and angered me.

I've yet to meet a compulsive gambler who isn't intelligent. It's a prerequisite, along with the ability to be devious, manipulative and a top-quality liar. Lies are needed to help feed your addiction, scam the necessary money and keep the other half off your trail. You have to be very dedicated to your addiction and pay it the attention it needs if you're to achieve your goals. My goals in life were very simple when I was young. I was convinced that I would be married by the time I was 25 and have three kids by the time I was 30. I'd probably have a steady job, and the wife would look after everything at home. I didn't think too much beyond that, to be honest.

No addict sets out in life wanting to be an addict. It doesn't look good on the CV. As I've gotten older, I've come to terms with the fact that I'm a compulsive gambler. I accept it, and acceptance is the key to getting better and restoring some manageability in my life. But I spent years fighting it. I would never admit, let alone accept, that I could not control my gambling. How the fuck could I be an addict? I'm an intelligent guy. Surely I can control myself and stop whenever I want. How could I have a problem with it?

But then, why was it that every Friday at 4 p.m., when I got paid, I found myself running down to the bookies, convinced that I was going to at least double my wages within the next hour? Every Friday … without fail. Why was it that by 6 p.m. a lot of those Fridays I'd be thinking about whether or not I'd put petrol in the car or back the winner of the last dog race at Monmore? What excuse was I going to give the lads for not going out this weekend because I was broke? Or where was I going to bring them all to celebrate a big win? The former much more often than the latter.

Albert Einstein is credited with saying, 'The definition of insanity is doing the same thing over and over again but expecting different results.' That sums up my life and the life of almost every addict.

Again, I challenge anybody out there to try and tell me that gambling isn't an addiction. There might be different types of addictions, but their cores are all the same, and their behaviours are identical in so many ways.

Easter 1989. Life is good today. I'm working in a factory where my dad is a manager. It's a new, vibrant factory that manufactures computers and employs almost a thousand people. My sister is also working here, and there's a great social aspect to it. There's a thriving sports and social club that's always having nights out, pub quizzes, sports days and more. I'm not working this weekend, and I'm going out with my girlfriend Caroline and her friends. That's not until tonight, though ... .

It's Easter Saturday. There's a great buzz around the town, as there always is at this time of year. People scrambling for the last of the Easter eggs and getting ready to go out on the town tonight. Around 2 p.m. I go to the Brazen Head, probably the hippest bar in town, for soup and a sandwich. This is a regular thing, and a group of us usually meet here at the same time every Saturday. It's an unwritten rule.

'Hey, Pat,' says Colin the bar manager.

Colin's a good guy, been working here for years. Everyone knows and loves Colin. Which is probably why I do. That, and the fact that Colin is a big punter. He loves a bet, and he knows his stuff.

'Hey, Col, any sign of Hughie or any of the lads?'

'Not today so far ... any craic?'

'Not a lot, Col ... not a lot.'

I take my usual seat, and Suzanne, the most gorgeous barmaid I've ever seen, brings me my usual soup (as long as it's not mushroom) and a ham-and-cheese toastie with her customary big smile. This smile would warm the heart of the coldest creature, but I put it to one side. *Suzanne is way out of my league, and the smile is just part of the job*, I tell myself. That, and the fact that I have a girlfriend.

It's really quiet. Colin joins me, *Racing Post* tucked under his arm. 'Fancy doing a Yankee between us?' he says. 'You pick two, and I'll pick two. Shur, it'll be a bit of craic, and it'll pass away the afternoon.'

'No bother,' I reply.

This excites me for several reasons, the betting being only a small one. Colin, the shit-cool barman that everyone loves, is treating me like I'm a good friend. This will do my image no harm at all.

He leaves the paper with me and heads back behind the counter to work. I start studying the form – although, truth be told, I haven't a clue what I'm reading. I might be gambling for a few years, but the reality is that I don't understand 'form' yet, and I back primarily favourites, simply because statistically they are supposed to have the best chance of winning. Because I now have the honour of doing a bet with Colin, I'm not going to pick favourites. I'm going to make it look like I know what I'm doing. I pick a 5/1 shot and a 3/1 shot. Horses that are kinda fancied, but not the favourites.

Colin asks me my choices and tells me his, which are a 7/2 shot and, surprisingly, a 6/4 favourite. We each stake £11, as there are 11 £1 multiple bets in a Yankee. We figure we should get two winners and get at least our stake back; plus, the last race we've bet on isn't until 5.05 p.m., so we'll get good value for our money.

The first race sees my 5/1 shot. It's a six-furlong sprint at Haydock Park. I'm watching with no pressure … this guy is the least likely winner of our four selections. My guy goes off in front. Colin and I both groan at this. The pacesetter rarely, if ever, wins a bloody sprint. Three furlongs are gone, and my guy is two lengths ahead. A sitting duck. I pick up the paper and start reading about Manchester United's latest transfer target and prepare for our second race.

The next thing I hear is Colin's fist slamming against the bar counter, causing the head to spill on my pint.

'Go on, my son, ride him out … go on, go on … use the whip.'

I glance up at the telly: there's half a furlong left, and my guy is still a length ahead.

'Yessssss!' I shout.

That's an unexpected great start. He wins, easily. Colin slaps me on the shoulder, winks at me and walks away with a wide grin on his face.

Next up, it's Colin's first choice. A 7/2 shot in a maiden hurdle at Leopardstown. No worries here. It's an all-the-way success, made easier by the fact that the two main rivals both fall early in the race. That's a 5/1 and a 7/2 winner we have. This means that, no matter what happens with the last two races, we're in profit as we have already secured £54 guaranteed from that double.

The next race isn't for an hour. I'm going for a walk down the town. On my travels, I pass Tony Connolly's, the best menswear shop in the city. In the window there's this awesome leather jacket. It's £179, though. Almost a full week's wages, but I'm due tax back in a few weeks. I'll have that jacket then. For sure. I call Caroline at work and make plans for tonight. Then I head back to the pub to see how we get on with our last two horses.

The bar is a bit busier when I get back. Shoppers are calling in for a beer or a coffee before they go home. I head for the end of the bar where we always sit; unsurprisingly, my seat is still there waiting for me. Colin is great at 'suggesting' other seats for non-locals who come in.

It's now 3.30 p.m. My second horse is going into the stalls and is ready to go. Ray Cochrane is the jockey; Luca Cumani is the trainer.

Both are excellent in their given fields. There's a hot favourite in the race, though – an odds-on shot. This means that he's really fancied, and it's probably the best horse in the race.

'And they're off!' cries the commentator on *Channel 4 Racing*. Colin joins me, and we are both glued to the telly. The favourite is lying handily in third place, tanking along. My guy is still there, though, a length further behind and going equally well. The favourite kicks for home, but Cochrane covers the move, and with a furlong to go, he moves up beside the hotshot. Amazingly, with 100 yards to go, I see the dark-blue silks of my jockey move ahead of the pale-green ones of the supposedly unbeatable favourite, and next thing I know, we have three winners up and already a profit of over £200 each. What a day.

Now, the agonising wait. It's just 3.40 p.m. Our last race isn't for another hour and a half. Some regulars are coming up to me, congratulating me, asking me about the chances of the fourth horse. 'How much will you get if the fourth horse wins?' If I had a pound for every time I'm asked, I'd be minted and wouldn't need to gamble. It's all well-meaning, but it's driving me insane. I want the race to be on *now*. This next 85 minutes is going to be excruciating. My mind is wildly racing. I'm pretty sure my blood pressure is going through the roof. My palms are sweaty. I have no interest in the pint that's taking forever to disappear in front of me. I'm not really listening to anything anyone is saying to me. I'm in heaven and hell at the same time.

It's 5.05 p.m. Here we go. Colin's second selection. The one that could potentially win us a small fortune. I have already convinced myself that it's going to be beaten. Colin is cool as a breeze. At least, he looks like he is. I have no idea what I look like, but if it's anything like how I feel, it will be like a crazy person in an asylum.

The race jumps off. It's a three-mile chase. Fifteen big fences, each fraught with danger, and at least six minutes of sheer hell lie ahead. I'd rather have my teeth extracted, without any anaesthetic. I'm pretending to watch, even possibly looking calm, but I'm not taking anything in. I see Colin getting agitated, occasionally grimacing, occasionally fist-pumping. *Why am I feeling like this? Something's not right. My head is spinning. Get a grip. Take a deep breath!* I say to myself, all the while not fully aware of even where I am.

Colin runs out from behind the counter. He gives me a high five and looks really happy. All of a sudden, it dawns on me.

We've done it. Four winners. God knows how much we've won, but it's certainly more money than I've ever had in my entire life. I start to relax. Colin stands a round for the bar. People are genuinely happy for us and congratulating us. All of a sudden, I find myself back in Bambury's, when I won my first real bet a few years ago. The £51 win. But this time round it's different. It feels like it was meant to be. Superior. I stand a round for the bar, too. After all, that's what big shots do, and today has pushed me into the big-shot league.

Colin goes to collect the winnings. When he comes back, he hands me £500. 'That'll keep you going until Monday,' he says. 'They don't have enough cash to pay us, but they'll get the rest when the bank opens.'

Including a bonus, that day we walked away with the princely sum of £2,478 between us. That may not sound like much today, but back in 1989, it was a serious wedge. The average wage wasn't even £300 a week, and we had won over two months' wages. I met Colin on Monday at lunchtime. We had coffee and relived the whole day over and over. Each moment recounted was embellished a little. We agreed to meet again the following Saturday and have a go at repeating the feat. In my mind, it was a sure thing. The euphoric feeling was still coursing through my veins, and it was likely to do so for a while yet.

Later that afternoon, on the bus home, a few old ladies commented about how much they liked my new jacket.

CHAPTER 4

n 1989 my gambling really escalated. The gambling was much more than a curiosity now. The big win earlier in the year with Colin seemed to give me an air of invincibility. My popularity was at an all-time high, which thrilled me. I had a pep in my step every morning, and my optimism knew no bounds.

I'll try and explain as best I can just how my mind worked at that time. I took a look at what I was earning from my factory job. I was taking home £188 a week, plus overtime. That's less than £40 a day for a five-day week. I believed that I would be able to turn a £20 stake into at least £80 every day. If I gambled for five days a week and stopped as soon as I hit my daily target, I would have a minimum weekly income of £400. Simple, right? I couldn't understand why everyone wasn't doing it. Of course, the reality turned out to be very, very different.

It didn't take long for my master plan to unravel. And the unravelling accelerated very quickly.

In the summer, I was arrested for the first time. I had become friendly with new neighbours, John and Mary, who were honest, decent people. One afternoon, while I was in their house, chatting about Ireland's chances of qualifying for the World Cup in Italy, I saw a chequebook lying idly on the countertop. After ensuring I was alone, I proceeded to remove the last cheque from the book, safe in the knowledge that it wouldn't be missed until much later, if at all. I made it out for £30, a minuscule amount, I thought. When it hadn't come to light after several weeks, I presumed that I had gotten away with it.

One morning, I looked out the window and saw a blue car with a big aerial on the roof pull up outside. Two big, burly men in suits came to the door. They introduced themselves as detectives, and I brought them into the living room. It really was a 'good cop, bad cop' thing: one was nice as pie, the other angry and aggressive. When they questioned me, I immediately caved in and admitted everything. They told me to report to the station the following morning to make a statement.

While I was scared of the consequences of this, what hurt me the most was seeing how my mother reacted. The shame of her son bringing the gardaí to the door was extremely embarrassing for her, and like all self-respecting Irish parents, she was worried about being the subject of gossip on the street. Added to this was the fact that she wouldn't be able to look her new neighbours in the eye for a very long time.

I went to the station, as agreed, accompanied by my mother. I gave my statement and was told I'd receive a court date later. The first thing we did was go to the bank, where Mam withdrew the £30 I had stolen to repay the neighbours. She didn't speak a word to me for the rest of the day.

Court came shortly after. I pleaded guilty and was given the Probation Act. This essentially amounted to a warning. I had to be a good boy for 12 months, or else further steps could be taken. But in the life of a compulsive gambler, 12 months is an eternity. And to someone with the scheming mind and desire for money I had, being good for 12 months was one hell of an ask.

Towards the end of the year, I lost my job at the factory. The official line was that they weren't renewing the contracts of temporary employees, but deep down I knew it was because of the increasing amount of time I was missing due to 'illness' or to attend 'doctor's appointments' – both code names for my being in the bookies.

I was gambling constantly. I broke up with my girlfriend, who had gone to America to work for the summer as an au pair. Caroline was the first relationship I'd had since my first love dumped me when I was 17. She didn't know whether or not she was going to come home from America – she thought she might live there permanently. We both decided that the long-distance thing wouldn't work and that it would be better for both of us to call it a day.

This upset me, though. But every cloud has a silver lining, or so they say. Being single freed me up to gamble with less of a guilty conscience, and to avoid the disapproving looks Caroline's mother cast in my direction when we bumped into each other in town. Also, now that I was no longer in a relationship, I had more time to hang out with the guys in the Brazen Head; more importantly, I could now spend more time in the bookies.

December came. I generally loved this time of year, with the build-up to Christmas and all that went on socially around this time. One of the guys from the pub, Harry, had become a pretty close friend. We drank together and went to matches together; while he had no interest in gambling at all, I still found him great company, and a suitable wingman whenever we would hit the bars and nightclubs.

We had tickets for the hottest gig in the country: the U2 concert on New Year's Eve in the Point Depot. These were like gold dust. Harry had worked as a bouncer in a few clubs, and a few months earlier he had been asked to work security at the shop when the tickets were going on sale. He was in an ideal position to get tickets, and he duly obliged.

We took the bus to Dublin that day. We checked into our

accommodation and then went for a few pre-concert pints and a bite to eat. The gig was electric. Afterwards, we were on a total high and went out on the town to celebrate the New Year. The next morning, I woke early, around seven o'clock. Harry was seemingly unconscious next to me. He always got bad hangovers, and last night he had drunk more than normal. New Year's Day is traditionally a big gambling day, with a lot of meetings on. It's a gambler's dream.

On one occasion several months previously, we were in the pub, and I needed to go to the ATM to get cash. Harry needed some too, so he tossed me his card, told me his PIN and asked me to get him some. From that point on, I knew his PIN, which I memorised. If I'm being honest, I did this because deep down I knew that, at some point, Harry would become a victim of my gambling habit.

I tried to rouse Harry, to no avail. That was my cue. I quietly went over to his jeans, which were thrown in the corner, and looked in his wallet. There wasn't a whole lot there, definitely not enough for me to enjoy a day's punting. I took his bank card and sneaked out of the room.

I remember the morning well. It was absolutely pissing down. I ran the few hundred yards to the ATM and helped myself to £180 of Harry's hard- and honestly earned cash. I ran back to the hotel, and it didn't come as a surprise that Harry was still in a coma-like state when I entered the room.

We had breakfast around an hour later, and then we went down to the bus station and caught the 11 a.m. bus home. We were back by 2.30 p.m., perched on our regular high stools in the Brazen Head, regaling everyone with details of the incredible set list U2 had belted out the night before, bragging about how good the seats were and how amazing the night had been.

I made excuses and slipped away some time around 3.15 p.m.

After all, there was still around an hour's racing left, and I had Harry's cash burning a hole in my pocket. The plan was as simple as ever: get in and use what I had stolen from Harry, turn it into a nice profit and then figure out a way to return his money without him ever noticing it was gone in the first place.

I was at home before 5 p.m. I barely had the bus fare back, and that was the princely sum of 35p. Now I was racked with guilt, completely broke and wondering just how long it would take for him to suss out what had happened. Would he just beat the shit out of me, or would he have me arrested?

Either option seemed fair.

CHAPTER 5

The 1990s had just begun. A new year, a new decade and many new adventures. My first adventure came in mid-January. Harry received his monthly bank statement and saw the withdrawal I had made. The good thing for me was that he was happy to put it down to a drunken mistake on his behalf. This would have been a major result for me. I didn't think that Harry's new girlfriend, Marian, would enter the equation or that her meddling (as I saw it) would land me in serious trouble.

It was Marian who encouraged Harry to check the withdrawal with the bank. The subsequent investigation led to them showing him CCTV footage of the transaction – and me, in full view of the camera, withdrawing the cash using his card. There was no lying my way out of this one. I had already dug myself a monster-sized hole by implying that it had probably been his own fault, a stupid drunken mistake. I was screwed, no two ways about it.

I first became aware that the game was up when I went to the pub.

I sat at the bar, waiting to be served, but I was ignored by both Colin and Suzanne. When I finally got their attention, they told me that I was no longer welcome and should find somewhere else to drink. I had never felt so embarrassed or low. I ran out the door as quickly as I possibly could. All I wanted at that time was for the ground to open up and swallow me whole.

A few days later, while walking into town, I was picked up by the gardaí and taken to the station, where I gave a truthful statement, admitting my culpability. Like before, I was released pending a court date. I was relieved that the arrest had happened on my way into town. This meant that they wouldn't be calling at the house, so I could hide what was going on from Mam. This was good for both our sakes: no shame for her, and no grief from her for me.

In the days leading up to my court date, I told absolutely nobody about it. I didn't want anybody to help me, or to even know. I became gripped by fear. Maybe fear isn't the right word. Paranoia certainly is. I was convinced that I had become persona non grata everywhere and that everybody was talking about me. I was convinced that it was going to be plastered all over the newspapers, and I was scared of ending up in prison. The thought of that petrified me.

As it turned out, I had nothing to worry about. My solicitor blamed my youth, inexperience and stupidity, and the judge put me on probation for a year. I had now progressed past the warning stage of probation to the under-supervision stage. There wasn't even a reporter in sight at the courthouse.

What was all the worrying about? I remember saying to myself.

However, I do remember the detective who played bad cop when I was arrested for stealing the neighbours' cheque being in court, and the looks of absolute disgust he kept throwing in my direction.

'You might be getting away with it for now,' he said to me outside the court afterwards, 'but mark my words, I'll be watching you like a hawk!'

I hurriedly moved away from him. He was an old-school cop with a reputation for getting a confession by any means necessary. I was sure that, if he ever did get to arrest me again, it wouldn't be pretty.

I went home as normal that evening, and nobody was any the wiser as to what had happened that day. This was a good result for me.

However, my life was changing at a pretty rapid pace, and people close to me, my family, were starting to notice. I was no longer heading out to the Brazen Head to meet Harry and the lads. I had reverted to hanging out with the lads I'd grown up with.

One thing happened at this time that I found very strange. My neighbours, the people I had stolen from, invited me into their home. I had presumed this was for the lecture – you know, the one where they'd tell me what a disgrace I was and that I should be ashamed. And there was a bit of that at the start. But then, John took an envelope out of his pocket that contained two tickets to an Ireland v England soccer match, and he asked if I wanted to go with him. He then told me that anyone can make a mistake – it's how you recover from it and learn that really matters.

I was completely overwhelmed by this. We went to that game, and many others thereafter. We became good friends, and we still are to this day. The ability to forgive is a gift from God. I've only been the victim of crime on two occasions: once, my apartment was burgled, and another time my car was broken into. I don't know who either culprit was, but I'm not so sure I would be so forgiving if I did. But my neighbours' compassion towards me certainly left me with food for thought. In a way, I was envious of their ability to forgive and the obvious inner peace they seemed to have.

Looking back now, I can see that my self-esteem issues have always left me unable to find this inner peace. They say that happiness comes from within. I'm still working on this, more than 30 years later.

Probation started well. I had a seemingly nice lady named Maura as my probation officer. For the first few weeks, I kept my appointments, engaged well with her and generally did as I was asked. This was, of course, all bullshit. I was playing the game, telling her all the things she wanted to hear and doing it very sincerely. She fell for it hook, line and sinker. Or so I thought.

The biggest lesson I learned from Maura and probation in general was that I wasn't as clever as I thought I was. Not everyone bought into my bullshit. This was a very new concept to me, but where a 'normal' person might learn from their mistakes and grab the opportunity they had been given by the courts with both hands, I still had an air of invincibility surrounding me. All the while I was caring less and less about myself. I had no regard for the consequences of my actions. 'Shur, Mam will bail me out and repay anyone I owe money to' became a familiar mantra.

One morning I had a meeting scheduled with Maura, but I didn't turn up. I had developed a scheme in my mind whereby I would scam the bank out of a few quid by telling lies. I would go to the bank(s) and tell them that I wanted to open an account because I was going to be selling a house I had inherited. I would then tell them that I needed a small overdraft to cover fees, and they would hand me out sums between £250 and £500. Of course, I never intended to repay them. I chose my banks a reasonable distance away from where I lived, so nobody would recognise me.

I must have pulled this stroke in four or five different banks. For some reason, it always worked. I would use the same patter, and because I was providing authentic identification and proof of address, there never seemed to be an issue. Almost 20 years later I decided to reintroduce this particular stroke to my repertoire, and it had pretty catastrophic consequences for me. You'll read about that later.

On the morning I was to meet Maura, I hitched a lift to the town where I needed to be to do the deed. When that was done, I headed straight to the bookies.

That evening, Maura called to my house. I invited her in and proceeded to give her a big spiel about being sick and not being able to get to the phone. She seemed to accept this until she gently told me that she had seen me hitching that morning on her way to work. Busted with a capital B!

She gave me an appointment for the next morning, stressing that I was really in the shit and had better not miss this meeting, no matter what.

The next morning, I turned up for my appointment 10 minutes early. I had prepared a variety of excuses the night before as to why I had missed my previous engagement, and I was pretty confident that Maura would buy into them. That was mistake number one. She didn't believe a word of it, and I was issued with an official warning: if I lied to her again, or if I missed another appointment without a valid excuse, she would have no hesitation in bringing me back to court and telling a judge about my lack of cooperation.

The shame of that lambasting and being caught out by Maura didn't last long. Within a few days, I was completely broke again and scheming about where my next scam would take place. I was living at home and didn't have to worry about rent. I wasn't working, but I wasn't signing on the dole either. I refused to do this out of sheer stupidity and pride. The dole was for life's losers, I thought.

My scheming was interrupted one Wednesday night when I was out watching a match at a nearby stadium. I was standing in the crowd when I felt a tap on my shoulder. I turned to find two gentlemen directly behind me. Detectives, but not any I recognised. One of them ushered me away, towards the direction of a nearby unmarked cop car. I got in the back; surprisingly, they didn't drive off but turned to me for a chat. They explained that they were from the same town I had previously visited to scam the banks. They told me what they knew, and that the game was up.

I had to attend the garda station the next morning. They indicated to me that the bank was not interested in having me prosecuted, but they wanted their money back. If that was forthcoming, I was in the clear. I told them I'd see them in the morning with a plan for repaying the banks. They seemed happy with this. I had fallen into deep shit yet again but had managed to come out of it smelling of roses.

This was too easy!

On my way back home, I felt happy. I seemed to have gotten away with a big problem, and yet again, I had managed to keep it from my parents. At least that's what I thought until I put the key in the door.

The minute I opened it, my mother was waiting for me.

'So, did you meet your two friends?' she said. I was completely in the dark.

'Yeah, Ray and Stephen were at the match with me. It was good craic. I'm off to bed now,' I replied.

'That's probably wise,' she said. 'What time bus are you getting down to Tipperary in the morning?'

The way she said this – she didn't even look up from the chair she was sitting on – told me the game was up.

I swallowed hard. It then dawned on me that the cops must have called to the house, and Mam had told them that I was at the match. Another hole dug for myself, I thought.

'It's not what you think,' I said.

'It never is,' she replied.

With that, I left the room and went to bed. It was a Wednesday night, so I knew that Dad would be in the pub. Wednesdays and Fridays were his nights. And I also knew that she wouldn't tell him. Another little secret between mother and son.

We went to Tipperary together the next morning. I made my statement admitting everything, and Mam went to the bank to get the cash to compensate the banks for their losses. Another £750. But I didn't care. It meant I was in the clear, free to gamble and steal with impunity. I was eating into Mam's life savings, but hey, *It'll all come good when I win big. I'll repay her 10 times over when that happens*, I told myself. Yet I could never bring myself to tell either of my parents about the true extent of my gambling, and how it was starting to own me.

It turns out that I didn't quite get away with it as easily as I thought. When looking through my file, the two detectives saw that I was on a probation bond. They put in a phone call to Maura, and I was summoned to see her.

'I see you've been a busy man,' she said.

I sat there with a confused look on my face. Then she told me about the phone call.

'Did you think you'd actually get away with it?' she asked.

'I've not been charged with anything. There won't be any charges because the money is repaid. It's all good,' I replied in my defence.

How wrong I was.

A few days later, I got a letter in the post telling me that I was being returned to court for failure to work productively with the Probation Service. I was pretty sure I was screwed this time.

The judge saw fit to sentence me to 240 hours of community service in lieu of a six-month sentence. I was still a free man. Just what did I have to do to get locked up? I might not have been a lucky gambler, but my God, I was one very lucky guy when it came to the courts. Community service – I didn't like the sound of that. Actual manual labour? Not for me. I was already planning on how to get out of it.

The by-now all-too-familiar letter – the one with the black harp on it, marked 'Probation Service' – came through the letter box.

> *Mr Sheedy,*
>
> *As determined by Judge O'Reilly at Limerick District Court, you are now required to complete 240 hours of community service, in lieu of a six-month prison sentence, effective immediately.*
>
> *Please report to David G****** at your local community centre to commence this order. Failure to comply will automatically result in a return to court to activate your prison sentence.*
>
> *Sincerely,*
>
> *Maura H*********
> *Probation & Welfare Services*

Great, I grunted to myself. *Just fucking great!*

The following morning, I made my way to the community centre and asked to speak to David.

'You're speaking to him,' said the guy behind the reception desk.

He looked more like the caretaker than the supervisor. He was scruffily dressed and had a very casual attitude.

'I'm here to start community service,' I said to him, not very enthusiastically. 'What does it involve?'

He seemed to appraise me, looking me up and down. Then he smiled and patted me on the shoulder.

'Don't worry, bud,' he said with a smile. 'It'll be all over in no time.'

I was allocated four hours a day, five days a week, for the next 12 weeks. I'd rather have had hot pokers stuck in my eyes. And I'm sure my attitude towards the work said as much.

After the first week was done, I realised it wasn't so bad. I was only doing one hour a day, and I'd spend the other three in the office with the other lads playing cards. The reality was that Davey, as we had been told to call him, didn't give a fuck who did what. As long as our timecards were stamped correctly, we could do as we wanted. After two weeks, I didn't even bother to attend anymore, except on Friday mornings to ensure my attendance card was stamped.

At the end of the 12 weeks, Davey sent a final report to Maura stating that I had completed my hours and that I was punctual and a very hard worker. She complimented me and told me that she was happy with my progress. I still don't know how I kept a straight face throughout it all – both my meeting with Maura and the entire 12-week community service period.

It was just another example of me falling on my feet again. The community service debacle had just served to make me feel even more like the human equivalent of Teflon. Nothing stuck to me, and no matter how awkward the situation, I just knew I was going to escape it.

CHAPTER 6

Around the summer of 1990, I was skimming through the Situations Vacant section of the local newspaper when I was struck by an advert by a Dublin-based company – let's call it The Liffey Aid Society. They were seeking a fundraiser to generate revenue for a housing project they were looking to expand. The ad said that they were looking for an 'innovative, dynamic salesperson capable of working alone and on their own initiative'.

Look no further, I said to myself.

I went through two interviews, and by the end of the second, I was offered the job. A low basic wage, decent commission and expenses were the remuneration on offer. I jumped at it. To be honest, the most attractive aspect of it all was that I was responsible for collecting all pledges made, which meant it was my job to send the money to the head office every month. Any compulsive gambler will tell you that this is their idea of heaven.

I worked hard, strongly motivated by the thought of getting my hands on all that cash. I did well, too. I found that I had a natural flair for selling and that I was a good enough judge of character to know what had to be done to get the customer to sign on the dotted line.

Several months went by. I was entering false figures every month. These figures made it look like I was just about meeting my targets, and the money I was sending each month reflected this. The reality was that I was not declaring at least two or three accounts every month, and I was keeping their contributions. I was always able to sweet-talk some clients into paying in cash. I always issued a receipt, of course. On average, I would collect contributions of between £20 and £50 from businesses and yield £200 a day. I would pocket £50 per day of this and stop off at Bambury's bookies on my way home to try and make my dreams come true. I rarely won, if ever (and if I did, it might have been only £100), but the belief that one day I was going to win big always kept me coming back.

As with all door-to-door fundraising, there's always going to be a member of the public that's suspicious. This job was no exception, and one day a Good Samaritan notified the gardaí that there was a suspicious character purporting to be from Liffey Aid trying to solicit funds on their behalf. I was apprehended on the street and asked to the station for questioning. I was petrified, my paranoia already screaming at me that the game was up.

The game wasn't up. I was asked to produce my permit and identification, which I did. The gardaí told me to wait while they sought verification. Around 20 minutes later, the officer came into the holding room and told me that everything was in order and that I could go. I felt the blood returning to my face, thanked the officer and got the hell out of there as quickly as I could.

At home that evening, I contemplated the situation. I got a call from my boss telling me not to worry, that in this line of work there would always be public suspicion, and that it was par for the course. My next phone call with him wouldn't be as kind.

Word spread around the gardaí that I was working as a fundraiser. The lovely detective I previously referred to as 'bad cop', the one who had threatened me outside the courthouse, decided to do the public a service and notified the company of my colourful past and my criminal record to date.

Shortly after, I received a call summoning me to the head office and telling me that I was to bring all literature, receipt books and business cards with me. The meeting was short and sweet. I was told I should have been honest with them from the start, blah blah blah. My employment was terminated with immediate effect. But it didn't end there.

The company decided to take a more forensic look at my work and quickly exposed the frauds that I had carried out. I was found to have stolen £625. In reality, I think it was higher but can't be sure. I was arrested when I got back home the following day. I made full admissions because I just wanted to get out of that station – being there gave me the creeps. I hated police stations: the smell, the atmosphere and the general feeling of impending doom they always gave off. I went straight home, again telling nobody about the strife I found myself in.

3 January 1991. A Wednesday that I'd remember forever.

I was told to be in court at 2.30 p.m. The detectives involved in charging me were fairly sound. They told me that they'd speak up for me and tell the judge about my cooperation. They told me I had nothing to worry about and that I'd be back home in no time.

In court, they were true to their word. The detective giving the evidence dumbed down the situation, and he did indeed begin to speak up for me. I started grinning inside. *Yet another victory is approaching*, I thought to myself.

Then the wheels came off – and, boy, did they really come off.

The detective's boss stood up to address the court. He cut off the officer giving evidence in mid-sentence.

'Your Honour, if I might address the court?' he said.

The judge dismissed the detective from the witness box and invited his boss to take the stand in his place.

'I solemnly swear that the evidence I give will be the truth,' he said.

'State your name for the court,' the clerk asked him.

'Detective Inspector Barry, Mary Street Garda Station,' he replied.

I knew from the look in his eye that something was wrong. For the next 10 minutes, I listened in horror as he read out in detail my previous convictions and told the court that I was a scheming, manipulative conman, a real menace to society.

The judge instructed me to stand.

'You have been given several chances by the courts. You have failed to take them. You have shown a blatant disregard for the law, and the probation services that have tried to help you. I sentence you to 15 months in prison.'

The whole room went white. I didn't know what was after happening. The next thing I knew, I was being taken away by two prison officers and brought to a holding cell behind the courtroom. My solicitor came back and advised me that I could appeal the decision and get bail pending said appeal. This meant that an independent surety had to come to court, be approved as suitable and pay the £500 bond. I immediately asked him to contact home.

Court had ended at 5 p.m. The two detectives who had told me everything was going to be alright escorted me up to the prison. They were quite apologetic and seemed to feel genuinely sorry for me.

When we got to the prison, the reality of my situation dawned on me. And it didn't feel good. I was booked in and placed in a holding cell. The two hours that subsequently passed seemed like an eternity.

Eventually, an officer came and brought me to an office. The first thing I saw in the office was my mother, sitting on a bench. Her expression was a mixture of tremendous anger and complete disappointment. I would rather have been stabbed in the gut than see this expression. I signed bail forms, and we took a very silent taxi ride home.

My father was waiting for me when I got in. I ran to my room to escape the bollocking and potential beating I expected. He came up after me and laid into me, but only verbally. I didn't really care about this, but the look on my mother's face still haunted me.

It was all crowned off on the following Friday when details of my arrest, charges and imprisonment made column inches on the front page of the local newspaper. My whole world was as good as over. Now everyone – and I mean everyone – would know who and what I was. I didn't know what to do. And I had nobody to turn to. I had burned all bridges available to me. I was at the lowest ebb yet in my nearly 22 years on this earth.

The months that followed were hell. I retreated into a shell, mostly because of the shame and embarrassment I had brought raining down on my family and myself. But it didn't stop me gambling. That was my escape, my solitude, and *nothing* was going to take that away from me. I still enjoyed the escape of a few hours in the bookies. Having swallowed my pride, I had signed on to the dole, but I just gambled the money as soon as I got it and then gave

Mam sob stories to get more money from her. I was also selling small things like my record collection and books to second-hand shops. It was very sad and desperate.

Back when I was on probation, Maura had wanted me to engage with mental health services. I had been able to admit to her about my gambling problem, and she was surprisingly understanding and supportive. She had enlisted me with the services, but the Health Board (now known as the HSE) was an even bigger mess back then than it is today, and as a result, I only received my first appointment in the summer of 1991.

I went for a few appointments. To be honest, the only reason I did this was because it would look good when my appeal against the severity of my prison sentence came up. At one of these appointments, I was told that a new treatment centre had opened about 25 miles away from my home. It was a 30-day residential programme, and it cost a fortune. However, they would accept a 25 per cent down payment and the rest in instalments. Of course, I wouldn't be the one paying for it. I returned to the well that was my parents' hard-earned money for that.

I went for an assessment. Mam came with me. She was watching me like a hawk those days. This was a family-based programme. You couldn't enter it unless you had family support, so it was imperative that she be there.

I passed the assessment with flying colours. I definitely had a problem. If you ticked 7 boxes out of 20 questions, you had a potential problem. Over 10 was a definite problem. I ticked 19. The only box I didn't tick was the one that asked about contemplating suicide. As life degenerated, that box would eventually be ticked as well.

Since it was a new centre, there was no mad waiting list. I could go in the following week. It was mid-September. My appeal was scheduled for the end of October. I had to do a really good job in here. My freedom depended on it. My gambling future depended on it. It was game on.

CHAPTER 7

When I got to the treatment centre, the first thing that struck me was how remote it was. It was literally in the middle of nowhere. The next thing I noticed was that I was the youngest there – and by a long, long way. I was 22; the next to me age-wise was at least 45. And they were all alcoholics and drug addicts.

What the hell am I doing here with these people? I asked myself.

I felt sorry for them. In a way, I was looking down on them, almost as if I had a superior addiction. I wasn't coming home drunk, beating up my wife or kids. There weren't track marks on my arms from needles. My air of superiority was still very much with me.

When being assessed for suitability, I met a lady named Mairéad who ran the centre. She had gone through the assessment with me and spoken to me in general about where I was in life. She asked why I was there, if I wanted to be there and what I wanted to gain from the experience. My answers were perfect, straight from the playbook. I told her that I was at the lowest ebb I had ever known, that I really wanted to be there, and that I wanted to gain enough knowledge and strength to use when I got home. I told her that I never wanted to gamble again.

The reality was, of course, entirely different. I didn't want to be there. I wasn't that bothered about learning anything because I was going to gamble again as soon as I got back home, and the biggest reason for being there was to get a favourable letter to show the judge at my appeal at the end of October.

Whether I liked it or not, I was stuck there for the next 30 days with some very crazy people. I was a fish out of water and was going to have to adapt quickly to my new environment if I was to survive and achieve my ultimate goal. It wouldn't be easy, but I'd been cheating and conning people all my life. This was just a different con. I needed to figure out a new strategy. It would need to be a good one in order to succeed: I was dealing with trained professional counsellors here, most of them recovering addicts themselves.

'You can't kid a kidder' is a phrase my dad used to say to me every time I'd try and squeeze a few quid out of him with a sob story.

We'll see about that, I'd say inwardly. *We'll see ...*

I was convinced that these counsellors wouldn't outsmart me. I'd play the game, only I would be the one running the show.

At any one time, there were 12 residents, both men and women, in the treatment centre, which had a revolving-door policy. When one person's 30-day stint was complete, they were discharged and someone else came in. I shared a bedroom with three other guys, all very different characters in their own right.

There was Paddy, a self-proclaimed raging alcoholic who had 'no desire to give up the drink' and was in treatment only to 'keep that auld bitch at home off my back'. There was Martin, also an alcoholic, who was cross-addicted to prescription medication. Martin was quiet and gave the first impression that he was a bit of a 'misfortune', as my grandmother would describe someone who seemed a bit thick. And then there was another Paddy. Paddy was an alcoholic who didn't belong in a treatment centre. It was as clear as the nose on your face that poor Paddy needed psychiatric help. He constantly gazed into the distance and never spoke to anyone outside of group sessions.

It was a very regimented place, not at all as I'd imagined. Every morning, we were awoken at 6.30 a.m. and expected at the breakfast table at 7 a.m. Then we had to wash up and prepare the dining area for dinner, which came at 1 p.m. A meditation session at 8.30 a.m. was followed by a group therapy session at 9.15. This lasted until 11.15, then we were back at noon for an unsupervised daily group meeting where we discussed issues among ourselves. The afternoons involved cleaning the kitchen after dinner, more group therapy sessions and a one-to-one session with your appointed counsellor. The day would finish with supper at 6 p.m.

My counsellor was an English lady named Theresa. A qualified addiction counsellor, she was married to a recovering alcoholic. I liked her from day one. She didn't judge me, and for some strange reason, she seemed to like me for who I was. I found that unloading my thoughts and secrets to her in our one-to-one sessions was very beneficial. However, I wasn't overly enamoured when she suggested that it was time for me to start sharing these thoughts in group, but that became inevitable after my first weekly family session.

Wednesdays were family days. Our family members would come down and be shuffled off into a room for their own therapy session in the morning. Mid-morning would come, and we were all put together in a big circle – all 12 residents and their family members. There were two counsellors present to mediate. Each family member was then encouraged by a mediator to confront their loved one with the truth about the devastation caused by addiction. And it wasn't pretty. At least mine certainly wasn't.

My mother is a generally quiet woman. Very private in lots of ways. For her, speaking in front of a room full of people about how badly her only son had turned out would be a very big deal. I was also pretty sure that she would dumb down or sugar-coat a lot of what was going on. I knew what made her tick, and I was pretty sure I had manipulated her enough over the years to make sure she didn't go the whole hog with the gory details of my life.

Boy, was I wrong.

She started off gently, with some small talk about how I used to steal from her and other little things. But just as I started feeling that things were going to be okay, one of the mediators, a guy named Mike, encouraged her to share what they had discussed earlier that morning. Bang! It was like being hit repeatedly by a truck for the next 10 minutes.

Mam let it all out. She remembered back to when I was a small child growing up in America (something I have very little recollection of – we came home when I was five), going into detail about things I had long forgotten. The time I saw a snake in the bushes in our garden, but nobody believed me until my sister came out and saw it too. The time I polished off the remains of all the beer cans at a barbecue and got drunk.

She spoke of how having the gardaí call to the front door made her a laughing stock in front of the neighbours. About how she felt when I pawned her wedding ring. About how it felt to not be able to afford the weekly groceries one time because she had bailed me out over something. But what hurt most of all was hearing the venom with which my mother spoke. It was the first time I had heard her speak from the heart, and it was devastating. I glanced around the room. There were looks of disgust from some of the other family members, looks of shock from some of my fellow residents and looks of disappointment from the mediators. Occasionally, I tried to defend myself, but each time, I was shot down by Mike telling me that I wasn't allowed to speak, only listen. I was reeling for a long time afterwards. Mam's words devastated me. But they also inspired me to do one thing: from that point forward, I was going to work hard while I was there, listen to my counsellor and shut up and do what I was told. That was a huge step.

Step One: We admitted we were powerless over gambling – that our lives had become unmanageable.

The 12-Step programme tells us to admit our powerlessness. I never had a problem admitting anything, but I did have a huge problem accepting it. There is a profound difference. Admitting something is easy. Words are cheap, and for somebody as manipulative as I was, it was easy to say the right thing at the right time. Acceptance, on the other hand, comes from within. I could always admit that I had a serious gambling problem. I couldn't accept, however, that it had owned me and that it was something I couldn't control. Until I found this acceptance, I was never going to get to the bottom of my illness.

Acceptance comes from within. It doesn't feel like anything, yet it feels like everything that's good. It's very hard to describe. If you asked 10 addicts what acceptance felt like, each answer would be different. But when you finally get it, it's magical. My acceptance was a long time coming: I only really accepted my lot when the steel door shut behind me on the evening of 14 October 2020. I felt like shit, but I also felt the weight of the world lifted from my shoulders.

Step Two: We came to believe that a Power greater than ourselves could restore us to sanity.

I also struggled very much with the spiritual aspect of recovery. In my eyes, spirituality meant religion. I was never a God-fearing type and I stopped going to mass at the age of 14. You are encouraged to 'hand things over' to a higher power. Theresa tried to explain the higher power concept to me, but it just wouldn't kick in. I was trying hard to make this thing work, but between the acceptance part and the higher power, I felt I was losing the battle.

Another humiliating Wednesday came and went, this time at the hands of my father. His tale was probably worse than my mother's the previous week. He spoke about the same things Mam did. They were seldom on the same page about anything, but they were in this. He spoke of the shame of reading about his son in the *Limerick Leader*, about me relieving him of his savings. The group didn't half let me have it in the sessions that followed. I started to retreat into myself. I was sharing less and less in group, and with Theresa. Then, something wonderful happened.

Mairéad came to me one evening after tea. It was a dull evening, already dark. She asked me if I'd like to go for a walk. There was a lovely path through the woods. I could only imagine how picturesque it would be on a summer's evening: the tall trees, the dirt path, wildflowers growing everywhere … it was almost like a movie set. As we walked, she asked me how I was doing and some other run-of-the-mill questions. We got to a bench at the top of the hill, and she asked me to sit. She took my hand and looked at me straight in the eye.

'How are you really doing?' she asked.

'Fine,' I replied. She smiled gently. She didn't believe me.

'Do you know what "fine" means in this business?'

'No,' I replied.

'Fucked up, Insecure, Neurotic, Emotional,' she said.

I looked at her like she had two heads.

'The first letter of each emotion.'

F.I.N.E. And it described me to a T.

I thought about what she said, and I understood. I opened up a little to her about my insecurities, my desires, my family and my feelings. And not once did she interrupt me. She continued to hold my hand, and she listened. Only when I asked her something did she speak. I didn't realise it, but I was in floods of tears, and it was only when I looked at her that I realised that she was also crying.

We sat there for much longer, and I poured my heart out. We laughed and cried, then cried some more. It was my first time crying in years. When we were finished talking, we stood up to go back to the house. Mairéad hugged me. To this day I can still hear her words:

'Learn to love yourself. You have so much love in you, but you waste it on people and things that don't deserve it. Love yourself first, then I promise you everything else will fall into place.'

There are very few people I can say have had a huge influence on my life. Sister Mairéad Kelly is one of those people. She is without a doubt one of the most selfless, loving people I have ever had the honour of meeting.

The days were flying by. Ever since I'd made the conscious decision to stop fighting with myself, I found that I could actually learn. I learned that it wasn't so bad to have red hair and glasses. It wasn't so bad being overweight. And, perhaps most importantly, I learned that I had a hell of a lot of arrogance and resentment in me.

Arrogance is a very dangerous trait in a lot of ways. It leads you to develop a false sense of superiority and an air of invincibility.

When you put 12 people together in one room, there are bound to be personality clashes. When you put 12 recovering addicts in one room, these personality clashes can resemble war zones. Nobody is safe. Lines are drawn, and sides are taken. In group therapy, an 'us against them' siege mentality often kicks in. Some are more eloquent than others, and they use their education and eloquence to condescend. These people often become group leaders: they are influential over other members of their group, and they are hated by members of the other group.

One day, Sister Mairéad called me into her office to tell me that I was indeed one of those people, and it shocked me to the core. If anybody had told me I was arrogant, I would have taken great offence and been deeply hurt. Not only did Mairéad tell me I was arrogant, but she also told me that I was very controlling of – in other words, I was bullying – other group members. You could have knocked me over with a feather duster. To hear these words come from her was devastating. I felt that all the progress I had made was a sham, that I hadn't learned anything at all.

That evening, I went for another walk with Mairéad. She explained to me what she had meant by her words earlier. Even when she was dismantling me piece by piece, pointing out actions that had led her to her opinion, she did so with compassion, and not once did it come across as criticism in any way. She made everything so clear and easy to comprehend.

I had bridges to build with people, me included. And I needed to start building straight away.

There was a Scottish lady in the group. Let's call her Nora. She was angry, feisty and a very dominant personality. Nora was the one I clashed with the most, and the one with whom I had to build the first bridge. It wasn't going to be easy: to say we seriously disliked each other would be a gross understatement. What neither Nora nor

I could see, albeit most obvious, was that we were two peas in a pod and that we shared the same addictive behaviours and flaws.

After teatime chores were completed, we had the evenings to ourselves. It being winter, the evenings were dark, so almost everybody stayed within the confines of the house. There was a TV room, and there was always a scramble for the remote control – the women wanting to watch *Coronation Street*; the men, anything else. This particular evening, there was a highlights programme of the day's play at the Rugby World Cup. Ireland had played a big game earlier that afternoon. I was mad to see the coverage, and all of us men in the house had deliberately avoided the final result on the news earlier. Unfortunately, there was also a cliffhanger episode of *Corrie* on at the same time. Something had to give.

I got to the TV room first, secured the remote and sat in the best seat in the house. I was very pleased with this outcome. A few other guys who were interested in the rugby arrived, and the scene was set. A few minutes later, the ladies, led by Nora, came in, only to be disappointed to see the rugby highlights on. Nora's disappointment, in particular, gave me a great thrill – the look on her face said it all.

The bitching started not long after. Barbed comments were flying over and back, with the women being particularly catty. Then Nora played her trump card.

'Ireland were beaten in the last minute,' she shouted across at us.

I couldn't believe she had ruined it for us. I was livid.

'You selfish bitch,' I shouted at her. With venom too. 'It's no wonder your husband wants rid of you.'

I was breaking a big rule here by divulging something that had been shared in a group session. She silently glared at me, and if looks could kill, I was already six feet under. The next thing I remember was an object flying across the room in my direction. The remote control. It had been resting on the coffee table.

Nora had hurled it at me with force and precision. Luckily, I had ducked just in time. Who wasn't quite as lucky was Paddy. He had been seated behind me, oblivious to all that was going on around him. The remote struck him right on the bridge of his nose and broke his reading glasses. You could hear a pin drop thereafter. The remainder of the evening was spent in silence, everybody seemingly shocked and, in Nora's and my case, embarrassed at the turn of events.

The next morning, the attitude at breakfast was quite sombre. There was very little conversation between anybody, with people almost afraid to voice an opinion. I, of course, held the moral high ground. I was a victim. I didn't throw anything. That lunatic bitch had lost the plot, and now she was going to have to pay the price. Or so I thought.

After breakfast, Nora and I were individually summoned to the office to speak to Mairéad. She listened to both sides, passing no comment or judgement throughout. After group therapy that morning, we were due to have a meditation class. As we were seated, Mairéad stuck her head in the door and called us both into her office together.

The first thing she did was hand each of us an envelope. In each envelope was a bill for an equal share of the cost of replacing the remote control and the cost of repairing Paddy's glasses.

'You cannot be serious!' I exclaimed indignantly. 'I wasn't the one that got violent, this isn't down to me.' I was standing firm. Nora just sat there, saying nothing.

'I suggest that you go for a walk together and see how you both feel when you come back.'

This was more of an order disguised as a suggestion, as only Mairéad could do.

Nora and I walked down the long driveway towards the exit gate. There was nothing said for the first part of the short walk. It was a misty morning, and neither of us had an umbrella. There were cows grazing in the field, and we fixed our gaze on these beasts, both of us reckoning that they were the lucky ones. All they did was stroll around, eat and sleep. They didn't have courts or guards or angry spouses outside that gate waiting for them. They didn't have bills or alcohol or gambling problems. Bastards.

We stopped and looked at each other, still no conversation. Then, almost in unison, we both started smiling. Then laughing. Then babbling apologies to each other so fast that neither of us could understand what the other was saying. For the rest of the walk, we poured our hearts out to each other. In the 30 days I spent in treatment, that one hour was one of the most beneficial to my recovery.

Mairéad had woven her magic yet again.

At the end of my 30 days, I said my goodbyes to everybody. To Theresa, my counsellor who had helped me build up my knowledge and understanding of my addiction. To all the residents who were still in the house. To Helen, the chef who had cooked so much wonderful food for me over the 30 days that I had put on at least a stone and a half. And, mostly, to Sister Mairéad. There would never be enough gratitude I could show this woman. She had changed my life in so many ways, and all of them for the better.

CHAPTER 8

Things felt strange when I got home. That's because things *were* strange. My life was going to be very different from the one that I had been living, or at least existing in.

I came home on a wet Wednesday. The reception was not the one I had expected. There was a curt 'hello' when I came through the door and little else. No welcoming party, no bunting, no cake. Deep down, I had known there wouldn't be, but a small part of me had hoped there would be.

The first decision I made when I got settled in that evening was that, after dinner, I would go to my first Gamblers Anonymous meeting. There had been a meeting in the treatment centre, but it had been an Alcoholics Anonymous meeting. I was told to go, even though I was not an alcoholic, because Theresa reckoned that I would be able to relate to a lot of what was going on with the people sharing. This had turned out to be true. The biggest thing I learned from the AA meetings was that all addicts have the potential to become cross-addicted and that the behaviours of all addicts can be very similar. The highs achieved may differ with alcohol, drugs or gambling, but the core of the addiction is very much the same.

The Gamblers Anonymous meeting was at 8 p.m. in a social services centre in town. I got the bus as close as I could and walked the rest of the way. When the meeting started, there were only five of us there. A man named Joe chaired the meeting, which lasted two hours. It was similar to the AA meetings in format, but the readings we did were relevant to gambling and came from *The Little Red Book of GA*, which is the equivalent of the Bible for a compulsive gambler. It fits in your pocket and carries a host of vital information such as the 12 Steps and Traditions, the Just for Today prayers and the 20 questions I was asked in my original assessment to enter the treatment centre.

At the meeting, I shared how I ended up there. Everybody seemed to listen, and I could see a lot of nods of recognition from the other guys. While listening to their sharing, I also found myself nodding. The big thing I took from my first-ever GA meeting was that I was not alone and that there were others out there like me. In a sad way, this gave me great comfort.

Tomorrow was going to be a very big day. I needed all the comfort I could get.

November 1991.

My day of reckoning in court had arrived. Today my appeal against the severity of my sentence would be heard, and I would learn my fate: freedom or incarceration. To say I was nervous was an understatement. I was sick to the pit of my stomach.

I got to court at 10 a.m. The hearing was scheduled to start at 10.30. I was sitting in the waiting area – my head in my hands, trying to ignore all of the hustle and bustle that was going on around me – when I heard something that made my heart skip a beat and caused me to look up. It was a familiar 'click-clack' sound. My mother's shoes. I'd recognise that sound anywhere. Although she had promised that under no circumstances would she ever set foot in a courtroom, she had come to support me. It took a lot of effort not to start sobbing there and then. This meant more to me than anything, and I knew I would be able to face what was coming a whole lot better now.

The hearing itself was short and sweet. The judge read reports submitted by the Probation Service, the treatment centre and the HSE psychiatrist I had been seeing. He addressed me and told me that, in light of my completion of treatment, he was prepared to give me a chance. He suspended the entirety of the sentence and wished me well.

I thought I was going to faint on the spot. I would have to engage with the services for another year, but that was the extent of my punishment.

On leaving the courthouse, I went to speak to Mam, but she just walked off at pace, seemingly angry at me yet again. I understood this, however. This was her way of venting at me. She was every bit as relieved as I was, but she wouldn't show it. The pain and stress I was bringing to her life were taking their toll.

When I got home that evening, I bought the *Evening Herald*. I needed to get out of Limerick, and I needed a job. The Sales & Marketing column in Situations Vacant had a whole host of possibilities. Tomorrow would be spent exploring them.

I awoke with a newfound pep in my step and a gamut of emotions: fear, trepidation, hope – and a little more fear thrown in for good measure. I made a couple of calls, only to be met by the same reply for all: 'Can you please fax your up-to-date CV?'

I hadn't prepared a CV for quite a while. I had written one out, but I had no way of typing it or printing it because I didn't have a computer at home. Unlike the present day, when every house has at least one PC, laptop or tablet, back in 1991 a computer was considered a luxury confined only to the affluent. I went into town and headed straight for a secretarial services office that provided typing and printing facilities. The girl behind the desk kindly agreed to fax copies for me. My job search had begun.

That afternoon I made some more calls. One ad in particular caught my attention: 'Advertising sales executive needed for European transport publication'. I called the number and was put through to a lady called Barbara. I told her that I had some advertising sales experience. To my amazement, she asked me there and then to go to Dublin for a few days for a trial. I literally jumped at the opportunity. We made arrangements for me to start on the following Monday morning and see how things went – no obligation for either of us to commit. I was nervous and excited at the same time. This, whatever it was, represented a new beginning. I'd been given a chance, and I was determined to take it.

CHAPTER 9

fter leaving the treatment centre, every morning I awoke with a prayer:

'God, grant me the serenity to accept the things I cannot change,
Courage to change the things I can,
And Wisdom to know the difference.'

Twenty-five magical words that always put me in a good frame of mind for the day. I also tried, albeit not very successfully, to meditate whenever I could.

I caught the mail train to Dublin on a cold November morning. It departed at 5.30 a.m. and was called the mail train because the post office used to send late deliveries on it every morning. It arrived at Heuston Station at 8 a.m. It didn't take long for things to go wrong.

I had bought myself a coffee at the station, and I had the bones of an hour to make the short journey to the office, which was on nearby Thomas Street. I decided to drink the coffee in the station, then ask for directions and stroll up. As it was a Monday morning, the station was packed, mostly with culchies travelling back to work, either in banks or the Civil Service for the majority of them. Eventually, I saw a seat on a nearby bench and sat. I had no sooner taken a large gulp of my coffee than, out of nowhere, a young lad ran past, picked up my rucksack and took off at a rate of knots. I jumped up to follow him but only succeeded in bumping into a lady and spilling my coffee over both of us. He was gone. And so were my clothes and most of my money for the week.

It took half an hour for the cops to come. They seemed to find what had happened amusing more than anything else. 'Stupid redneck,' I heard one say to his partner, who just looked at me with a silly grin on his face.

To be honest, I didn't care about the clothes or the money. I needed to get to the office for 9 a.m. no matter what. So I went to the nearest taxi rank, jumped in a cab and told the driver where I needed to be. That was mistake number two.

A journey that should have taken five minutes and cost no more than three quid ended up taking half an hour and costing a tenner. A typical stunt by taxi drivers when they hear a country accent, apparently. I was late for work, covered in coffee and had been robbed twice. Welcome to Dublin.

I finally reached the office. I had contemplated not going in at all and catching the next train back home. The omens were not good. I went to Barbara's office. She was my age, slightly goth in appearance and generally pleasant. I explained to her what had happened, and she seemed genuinely sympathetic. She told me how the business worked and what my trial entailed. I would be paid a basic wage for the week and 10 per cent commission on any sales that I made that were verified by the back office. I was happy with this, and she showed me to the sales office.

The office – in fact, the whole building – was pretty drab. It was quite old, in bad need of refurbishment, and there was an overpowering smell of hops brewing in the Guinness factory next door. But I loved the area. It oozed character. Street traders, the Liberty Market, old-school pubs and an excellent chipper. It felt right.

The ground floor of the office used to be a hair salon. There were gaudy mirrors on the walls and ridiculous lino on the floor. There were two sales reps seated at desks when I was brought in. Barbara introduced me to Corey, the owner's son, apparently, and an Indian guy called Dev. In the office, there was also a secretary who looked after all the admin. Annie was her name. It all made me feel at home, and I got stuck into work straight away.

Over the course of the day, I got to meet the girls in the production department. They were the ones who put the magazine together. Christina, the owner's daughter, wrote articles and was the general manager. Olivia was the typesetter, responsible for the layout and design. Barbara did a bit of everything and was the owner's right-hand woman. It was a small business, but a tight-knit one, and I was made to feel welcome.

The owner, a very ostentatious, brash character called Bob, introduced himself to me by phone. He was in Spain, apparently, where some of his business interests were based. He spent a lot of time travelling between Dublin, Galway and Spain. He was very jovial on the phone, shouting encouragement at me that I was going to do very well, and that he had a good feeling about me. To be honest, I thought he was a little crazy. I'd never encountered a business owner quite like him before.

I had booked a bed and breakfast in nearby Manor Street. I planned to stay there until Thursday when I had to go home for my aftercare meeting, something I would do every Thursday for two years as part of my treatment. It was also a condition of my court appeal.

When I got to the B&B, I explained to the owner what had happened that morning and that I wouldn't be able to pay her until Friday. It was £15 a night. She looked at the letter I had got from the gardaí about my bag being stolen, and she was fine with waiting to be paid. Normally, my mind would have been working overtime, scheming and plotting a way to get out of paying. But this time was different. Maybe I was learning after all? The room was nice, and the breakfast was sumptuous. I certainly fell on my feet there.

On Thursday evening, I got the train home after work and made it just in time for my first aftercare meeting. This was a group of 10–12 people who had finished residential treatment discussing how life had been since completion. Facilitated by two counsellors, it was an integral part of the treatment process. I got home around 10.30 p.m., had a brief chat with Mam (Dad was in bed) and retired. I had to be up early in the morning to catch the mail train to Dublin again.

By 3.30 p.m. on Friday, the office was winding down for the weekend. I had sold two small ads, and to my surprise, I was handed an envelope by Barbara with a pretty decent weekly wage in it. From Spain, Bob congratulated me on a good first week. He said he would see me next week and that I was now part of the team. I was elated. My new life was beginning, and it excited me.

Later, Barbara told me that Bob's first reaction when he heard of my plight on the Monday I started had been to 'throw him £50 and send the poor fella back home'. We were to work together for over 20 years.

I first met Bob on my second week in the job, when he returned from Spain. I had heard lots of stories about him in the office, some from his own children, who worked there. The first impression I got from these stories was that Bob was feared. Apparently, he had a temper. He was purely financially motivated, and if sales reps were performing well, they were handsomely rewarded; if they weren't, it was the polar opposite. Bob was also a recovering addict, addicted to both alcohol and prescription drugs. He had been clean and sober for more than 25 years, but he fully understood addiction. While in many ways this was an advantage for me, it was also a huge disadvantage. Bob knew exactly how to control everything around him, and at times that included me.

For the first few weeks of our relationship, Bob largely left me to my own devices. Because I was new at the job and eager to impress, I was at the office 10 minutes early every morning, and I'd always be the last to leave every evening. My sales were steady, if unspectacular, and my figures for the first month were actually quite good.

My first run-in with Bob came about as a result of drink rather than work performance. One evening, we were due to send a magazine to press, and the production department was behind schedule. Olivia asked if anybody would stay behind and help out. I had nothing better to do, so I stayed, along with Annie, the secretary. We were flying through the work, and Olivia said she was going for a cigarette. She returned about five minutes later with a tray of 12 bottles of beer from the pub next door and some munchies.

We were enjoying a beer after finishing when we heard the front door open. In walked Bob, together with his sidekick Paddy, a rather menacing individual who never said much but was always around. Soon after, I found out that Bob employed Paddy as a minder. When I asked why Bob would need a minder, one of the sales guys told me that Bob had pissed off a lot of people over the years, either by not paying bills or womanising. Paddy hung about in case there ever was an angry customer or someone's husband nearby.

'What the fuck is going on here?' was the angry roar from Bob. He was absolutely fuming. We tried to explain to him that we were working late to ensure the magazine reached the printers on time, but he wasn't having any of it.

'Get the fuck out of here now! How dare any of you bring drink into my office.' The voice was getting louder, and angrier. Needless to say, we ran.

The next morning, we relayed the previous night's activities to the rest of the office. It got a lot of laughs. Bob usually appeared at the office around 11.30 a.m., and that morning was no different. Instead of sticking his head into the sales office, he went straight upstairs to his own office on the third floor. This wasn't a good sign. If his mood had been good, he would have called in and given us all a brief motivational speech. Bad moods meant he went straight to his own office.

Around an hour passed when my phone rang. 'Ext. 22 calling' on the display meant Bob was on the other end of the line. In a low but clearly angry tone, I was summoned. I needed this like a hole in the head.

When I got to the office, I sat down opposite him and next to Christina, his daughter, with whom he had no doubt been discussing what had happened the night before. Nobody said anything for at least a minute. That minute felt like an eternity.

'I'm very disappointed in you,' Bob said to me, shaking his head in a very dejected fashion. It was almost like a teacher would look at their star pupil who had just done something silly. He then proceeded to give me a lengthy lecture about alcohol, his own struggle with it and its dangers. Caroline, beside me, was kicking me under the desk, trying her best to stifle a laugh.

I sat there, chastised, and apologised as sincerely as I could. I felt like telling him that he should be thanking me, given that I had worked an evening without overtime, just to ensure that the magazine went to press on time, so he could collect all of the outstanding advertising revenue that was due on it. But since this was my first run-in with him, I decided to keep my powder dry. He was laying down a marker, letting me know who was boss. And that was fair enough. We would have plenty of arguments over the next 20 years that would add fuel to what was to become a love–hate relationship.

Olivia and Annie weren't as lucky as me. As they incurred Bob's wrath, shouts and roars could be heard throughout the building. I was learning about my boss. It was now apparent that the only people, his own family included, he had time for were high-achieving salespeople. Note that I say 'time' and not 'respect' – Bob had no respect for anybody.

My ability to make money for him was my one trump card. Over the next two decades, I would repeatedly play it to get what I wanted. I was prepared to put up with whatever toxicity came from him. What did that say about me as a person, though? The answer: even after everything I had been through, I was still devoid of self-respect and driven only by my one true god.

Money.

CHAPTER 10

Dublin life suited me for a variety of reasons. Limerick was a city with fantastic amenities and nightlife, but Dublin was so different, in the Champions League as opposed to the Europa. There was always something to do, a superb infrastructure and, most importantly for me, nobody knew me. My past was mine alone, and people judged me on how they found me, not on gossip or newspaper articles.

I had got friendly with Olivia, the typesetter from work. She lived in a flat in Smithfield Market, just 10 minutes away from the office, with her boyfriend Gary. Gary was a hulk of a man, at least six feet five, burly and menacing. He worked as a bouncer in a pub in the city centre. He wasn't the sharpest tool in the shed, but I liked him. After a few weeks, the bedsit below their flat became available to rent. They put in a good word with the landlord, and next thing I knew, I had my first Dublin address: £25 a week, bills included. It was small, a little tatty and very basic, but it was *mine*. Things were slowly but surely getting better.

Another thing Dublin was great for was recovery. Any form of addict can go to multiple meetings every day, in a variety of locations. I found a couple of great GA meetings, on the Navan Road and Gardiner Street. I was going to three or four meetings a week, plus aftercare on Thursday nights. Initially, I had to go to Ennis for this aftercare, but they eventually found me a group in Dublin, in Glasnevin. My desire to gamble had gradually subsided.

When the urges came, I was able to pull my *Little Red Book* from my jacket pocket and read from it. The Just for Today section became very important to me. It teaches us how to live in the day, not to project or dwell on the past.

JUST FOR TODAY

Just for today, I will try to live through this day only and not tackle my whole life problem at once. I can do something for 12 hours that would appal me if I felt that I had to keep it up for a lifetime.

Just for today, I will be happy. This assumes to be true what Abraham Lincoln said, that: 'Most folks are as happy as they make up their minds to be.'

Just for today, I will adjust myself to what is and not fit to adjust everything to my own desires. I will take each day as it comes and fit myself to it.

Just for today, I will try to strengthen my mind. I will study. I will learn something useful. I will not be a mental loafer. I will read something that requires effort, thought and concentration.

Just for today, I will exercise my soul in three ways: I will do somebody a good turn, and not get found out; if anybody knows of it, it will not count; I will do at least two things I don't want to do, just for exercise; I will not show anyone that my feelings are hurt – they may be hurt, but today I will not show it.

Just for today, I will be agreeable. I will look as well as I can, dress becomingly, talk low, act courteously, criticise not one bit, not find fault with anything, and not try to improve or regulate anybody but myself.

Just for today, I will have a programme. I may not follow it exactly, but I will have it. I will save myself from two pests: hurry and indecision.

Just for today I will have a quiet half-hour all by myself and relax. During this half-hour, sometime, I will try and get a better perspective of my life.

Just for today, I will be unafraid. Especially I will not be afraid to enjoy what is beautiful and to believe that, as I give to the world, so the world will give to me.

Just for today, I will not gamble.

Christmas 1991 in my house was a memorable one for me. It was the first Christmas I had in adulthood when I wasn't consumed by money and materialism. I had a job with prospects, new friends (that I have to this very day) and no bouts of panic whenever I saw a police car approaching. My dedication to recovering from the damage I had done to myself and others was going well. I was enjoying my meetings and my aftercare; most importantly, the relationships I had ruined the most, those with my parents, were slowly mending. Life was on the up, and the '90s became a very memorable decade for me, entirely free of gambling, crime and court appearances.

Perhaps there was a life out there for me after all?

*

If I were to write about everything that went on in my life, I'd never finish this book. As I said, the 1990s for me were great. I went on my first-ever foreign holiday, the first of many. I went to Spain with Podge, a good friend I had known since childhood. Bob, my boss, owned a cabaret club in Fuengirola and gave us the use of an apartment for a week. We had a ball.

I was also able to start fulfilling a few bucket-list things, which I would never have done when gambling because I would have blown every single penny I had, and more. I regularly went to Manchester United matches, including that incredible night in Barcelona in 1999, when they so dramatically won the Champions League.

I was also able to get involved in rugby union. As a sport, rugby became fully professional in 1995. Some friends of mine from home were top-class rugby players, and they were being headhunted by leading clubs in England. One friend asked me if I would accompany him to a meeting with one of these clubs, Saracens FC, and observe. He was not at all business-minded and feared that his enthusiasm to play professionally could compromise his ability to look at any offer objectively. Basically, he didn't want to get screwed over.

We flew to London for the meeting, which took place in the offices of a business owned by Nigel Wray, who also happened to own Saracens FC, a leading English club that was keen to be at the head of the queue when it came to professional recruitment. The meeting went well. So well that, within an hour of its conclusion, I received a call from Mr Wray offering terms that included a very generous salary, a fantastic bonus scheme, a top-of-the-range club car and accommodation. We were ecstatic.

Upon returning home, the deal, which saw my mate becoming only the second Irishman to play professional rugby, was all over the sports pages. My friend told a lot of other guys about what I did, and next thing you know, I'm representing at least six of the country's leading rugby talent. I ended up negotiating deals for them with clubs like Saracens, Harlequins, Bristol and Bath. I had toyed with the idea of quitting the job and doing this on a full-time basis. It would have paid very handsomely, and the perks were very appealing.

I did an interview with the rugby correspondent from the *Sunday Tribune*. The paper ran a two-page spread on me, complete with a posed photograph taken in St Stephen's Green. When I got to work the following day, Bob let me know in no uncertain terms who paid my wages. He also told me that he was concerned that this 'rugby shite' was interfering with my work and that perhaps I needed to decide what I wanted to do. In truth, I was too fond of the life I had built for myself and wasn't going to give it all away on a whim. But I used my new-found negotiation skills to my advantage. In return for committing to Bob, I was given a decent pay rise and a brand-new company car. My first-ever set of wheels.

A big contributing factor was the opinion of my GA sponsor and also that of my addiction counsellor. My sponsor was very pragmatic: he reminded me of where I had been at the height of my gambling and where I was now, and he focused purely on the importance of knowing where my bread was buttered. My counsellor was equally pragmatic but more compassionate. She focused more on what the positives were, what kind of future I could have and if I was happy with my lot. She reminded me not to be overly ambitious since this would be a trigger to a relapse.

They were great when it came to keeping me on an even keel. As well as my recovery was going, I still had the capability to self-destruct. The good job, the nice car and the high life all served from time to time to inflate my ego, and I still suffered from bouts of grandiosity. People were looking up to me – and at me – in a way that I had always desired, and I have to say that it provided me with a huge high. I wasn't gambling, I didn't need to, yet I still had all the things I had wanted from life.

'I have no desire to suffer twice – in reality and then in retrospect.'

This is another little adage that I picked up along the way in recovery. It was something I said to myself quite regularly throughout the '90s. Even though I was not gambling, even though I had all the materialistic things I used to crave and even though I wasn't in any trouble, I was aware that something was missing. I just didn't know what it was. I was still fearful – of what, I wasn't sure. I would go to a meeting, share about all the bad times and then about how I turned my life around. I became a poster boy for GA. I sponsored people in the fellowship. A sponsor is a mentor of sorts, who works through the 12 Steps with somebody who is struggling or is just there at the other end of the phone or in front of a coffee cup. From the outside looking in, I seemed to be in full control. Inside, while I was much better and still working hard at my recovery, I was still a mess in many ways.

The main thing for which I was grateful to recovery was the way it helped me rebuild the bridges I had burned with my family.

My father and I always had a strained relationship. I blamed him for a lot of my shortcomings. I now know that this was hugely unfair. My father was a Trojan worker. He worked hard all his life, and rarely if ever did I see him miss a day's work. During our arguments, I would take the moral high ground a lot. I felt fully justified in doing so. I constantly told myself that I was not going to grow up like him, no matter what. I wouldn't be a drinker, I wouldn't fight with my wife, and I would make sure my kids had a great life. Sadly, I didn't grow up like him. The truth of it is that if I had grown to be one-tenth of what he was, I would have been doing well.

Dad was born into a large family in County Clare. He met my mother when they were both working in a textile factory in Shannon in the early 1960s. They married in 1966, and my older sister arrived the following year. Shortly after I was born, in 1969, we emigrated to South Carolina, where skilled workers in the textile industry were sought. We lived there for six years, returning to Ireland in 1975.

I remember being taken to Thurles on summer Sundays for big hurling matches. There was always a great atmosphere and banter in the house when Limerick played Clare. Dad was a terrible loser, though, and he couldn't take the slagging that would follow yet another Clare defeat. When Clare beat Limerick in the 1995 Munster final, he cried. I was 26, and this was the first time I had seen any emotion come from him. The following September, when they won their first All-Ireland in 81 years, I cried in the Cusack Park stand with him.

I couldn't have had that moment with him had I been gambling. I would not have been able to afford the tickets, to put him and his brother up for the weekend of the match or to sit back and watch them celebrate like teenagers.

Thankfully, I was able to celebrate many more sporting victories with my father. Clare won the All-Ireland again in 1997, we travelled throughout Europe following the Munster and Ireland rugby teams, and he came to United games at Old Trafford, too. Seeing as he indoctrinated me as a small child to all things Manchester United, it was great to be the one who brought him to their home for the first time.

We had many, many bad times over the years, but I will always have the great memories we built along with those bridges.

My relationship with Mam was different from that with Dad. She would argue with me in private, but rarely if ever in front of anybody. I was her boy. When Dad or my sister would castigate me for being a constant source of shame to them, Mam would take my corner. Both of my sisters and I have very different relationships with her to this very day. I can't count how many times I broke her heart and her wallet. Inside our four walls, all hell would break loose whenever I was up to my old tricks. There would be screaming, shouting, deathly silence and sadness. But if anybody outside those walls tried to knock me or put me down, then they'd have to deal with her. She defended me to the last. It was all she knew; a strong maternal instinct, I suppose.

While I was able to bond with my dad through sports, the only way I could really make Mam happy was by not being in trouble, working and generally being happy. That's why we had such a good relationship throughout the 1990s. I'd take her shopping to retail parks where the buses didn't go. And, very importantly, I was always on hand should any of the family pets need to go to the vet. She adores cats. The walls at home are adorned with pictures of all the pets we ever had. They say that a person's nature can be assessed by how they treat animals. Mam's good nature can never be called into question.

Another big highlight of the '90s was the wedding of my older sister in July 1999. I was able to chauffeur her and my new brother-in-law around for the day in my company car. Things I could never have thought about having or doing had I not been on a recovery path.

Life was very good. Almost too good, perhaps, and for an addict, complacency is commonplace.

CHAPTER 11

saw in the new millennium in a great way: surrounded by friends and family, debt-free, bet-free and in a pretty good headspace. I had been promoted at work and was a member of the senior management team. I had overall responsibility for the sales and marketing department. I had a nice apartment in an affluent area of town, a top-of-the-range car and a pretty high social standing. There were constant invites to product launches, complimentary match tickets and gala balls.

Female company was never an issue for me. I didn't quite know what I wanted in the way of a love life. I had several relationships, some more serious than others, but none that had made me want to settle down. I had a great work–life balance: Monday to Friday involved work, mostly in Dublin or abroad. My weekends involved me going home to hang out with my friends or going to a match somewhere with them. I really liked this, and it was the cause of some relationships breaking up. I wanted to have my cake and eat it, too. I was living a bachelor lifestyle and enjoying every minute of it.

I was almost 10 years without a slip into my recovery. I still felt strong, but I was going to only two meetings a week, as opposed to four or five. My contact with my sponsor had also diminished, and not through his fault. I was still very cognisant of my addiction, but in hindsight, I can see that I wasn't giving my recovery everything it needed to survive.

My counsellor once told me that falling off the wagon can happen at any time, even to the strongest of recovering addicts. She also warned me that my disease (gambling) would be with me for life. There was no cure, but there were ways to control it. And I wasn't doing *everything* I could to control it. I was letting some of the old habits creep back in. Grandiosity and arrogance have always been my two main triggers, and I was starting to allow them back into my life. I kept telling myself that I was strong enough to deal with it, that it was just a blip.

I was wrong. And my fall from grace would be catastrophic.

Definition of a higher power:

> *A spirit or being (such as God) that has great power, strength, knowledge, etc., and that can affect nature and the lives of people.*

In treatment, you are taught to become as spiritual as you can be. It is an essential part of a successful recovery. This is something that I have always struggled with. I found it very hard to differentiate between religion and spirituality. Being able to 'hand everything over' to your higher power helps you deal with your issues and tells you that you are not alone in your recovery.

In 1991, when I came out of treatment, my higher power was God. This is because I believed in God, but I could not quite believe in the concept of a higher power. In my opinion, God is the supreme entity, the be-all and end-all. A higher power is a very personal thing, not necessarily a person, and something that you are prepared to hand yourself completely over to. I couldn't quite get this, so I chose God. I prayed to him whenever things got tough, and because my life had improved as much as it had, I was happy to believe that God was helping me. But in late 2003 things had changed. My recovery was wavering, and a family tragedy led me to question just where the fuck my higher power was when I needed him.

In 2003, my younger sister became pregnant with twins. I was delighted for her, and myself too. I already had a gorgeous godchild (my niece) and a new nephew, both born to my older sister. In November 2003, complications set in around the pregnancy that caused my sister to be hospitalised. While she was in the maternity ward being checked out, there were further problems brought about by negligence. As a result, the twins were born very prematurely. A beautiful boy and an even more beautiful girl, David and Katie came into the world early, both weighing in at little more than 16 ounces each. To put that into perspective, a bag of sugar weighs 32 ounces. They were the combined weight of a bag of sugar.

The week that followed was incredibly traumatic. Both David and Katie struggled very badly, the extent of the damage brought about by their premature births as yet unknown. Katie was the strong one. She fought and fought and hung on in there. Unfortunately, it all became too much for David. He passed away after a week-long battle.

The numbness that we felt as a family was palpable. It certainly led me to question my so-called higher power. How could anyone let this happen to a newborn child? We were all bereft. I couldn't even imagine how my little sister was feeling. She was left with loss, devastation and health problems as a result.

Katie was diagnosed as suffering from a condition called hydrocephalus. This is caused by an accumulation of cerebrospinal fluid within the brain. This typically causes increased pressure inside the skull. To this day, Katie needs a shunt to drain away excess fluid from her brain, she is deaf and has impeded speech.

Over the past 20 years, I have seen her grow into the beautiful young woman she is today. She attends third-level college, where she receives the most excellent education. She has a very good quality of life. She bosses her kid brothers around as only a big sister should. Thankfully, it's been a few years since she has been sick as a result of her condition. I can recall her lying on a hospital trolley after a seizure about 15 years ago. That wasn't the first one. Her entire life has been a series of battles, and she's won them all, no matter what gets thrown at her.

I have two higher powers today. My dad in heaven is one; the other is Katie.

CHAPTER 12

Very few addicts that slip do so on the spur of the moment. It is usually the result of a chain of events that have slowly but surely eaten away at them over time. It is quite often dramatic; if it were a piece of art, it would be loud, colourful and explosive. Mine was no different.

To this day, I cannot identify one particular thing that made me have that first bet in almost 13 years. I do know that my recovery had been taking a beating for several months. I no longer got the same satisfaction I used to from attending a GA meeting. I was listening to the same thing over and over again. Similarly, I was sharing the same stories all the time at meetings. I could tell you what a group member was going to say before they said it. There was a guy who shared every time about how, on the way home from a big gambling session, he often wouldn't have the money for the €1 burger in McDonald's. He would be known as The Euroburger in my mind.

Other characters earned monikers known only to me: John the Breadman, Billy the Burglar and Dennis the Menace, to name a few. I'm pretty sure they each had a nickname for me, too, because at this stage I had shared on several occasions every story that I was willing to share with a group.

I had saved a decent amount over the years. I never had any plans for this, like most normal folk would have. I didn't need a nice car because I had a company one. I didn't need a house because I was single, with no kids. I didn't invest my savings because there would be risk attached to investment, which technically would be gambling.

One afternoon in late 2003 I was walking up Thomas Street in Dublin. I had finished work and was returning from the chemist. There was a Ladbrokes betting shop at the start of Thomas Street, just beside where the Vicar Street concert venue is today. As I walked past, the door was ajar, and I saw the crowd in the shop. It looked so different from the last time I had set foot in a bookies almost 13 years previously. There was a multitude of large flat-screen televisions on the walls. There were leather armchairs all over the shop. There was a water cooler and a tea- and coffee-dispensing machine. I could almost feel the hairs standing on the back of my neck, and I felt slightly nauseous at the same time. I stopped myself from going in and started to walk briskly towards my car, wanting to get out of there as quickly as I could.

I didn't get far. In fact, I didn't even get 100 yards before I turned around and walked straight through the Christmas shoppers, eager to get through the betting-shop door and sample this new, modern-day gambling experience.

When I got in, I soon familiarised myself with the layout of the shop. I found out where the greyhound form was posted and headed straight for that section. The daily horse racing was finished, but the dogs always ran later. I looked in my wallet and saw around €250 in cash there. The first thought that came into my head was, 'I'll turn this into a grand, then go home. It'll only be a one-off.'

When I was gambling before, my betting patterns had always been around the £20–£30 mark and never higher than £50. To some people, this was huge, to others, a drop in the ocean. When in treatment, every addict is warned that their addiction will always be alive within them. You never beat addiction, but you do learn to control it on a day-to-day basis. If an alcoholic who built themselves up to drink a bottle of vodka a day stopped drinking for a long period, they would drink at least a bottle a day on their return to drinking, and quickly end up drinking more. It's the same for a drug addict with coke or heroin and a gambler with their next bet. You pick up where you left off, you don't start from scratch.

My first bet that day was €150 on a greyhound.

It will come as no great surprise to anyone that I left that bookies around an hour later with nothing in my wallet. On my way home, in the car, I distracted myself by calling Mam, listening to Eamon Dunphy's *The Last Word* on Today FM and generally trying to think about anything else other than where I had been for the last hour.

It didn't work. I felt physically sick and nearly vomited on at least two occasions. It wasn't the money. That was nothing, I still had plenty of that and a good job with great benefits. It was a combination of shame, self-loathing, fear and paranoia. I called my sponsor, and we met for coffee. I was going to go to a meeting. It would be alright, wouldn't it?

That night I didn't go to my regular meeting where I was well known. My ego wouldn't allow me. How could I walk into a meeting that I had been attending for almost 13 years and tell people who looked up to and respected me that I had slipped?

Instead, I found a meeting in another part of town. I had thought about not sharing at all, but eventually, I did. The support and feedback I received that night were incredible. I had tears in my eyes as everybody in the room clapped after I poured my heart out. That would be the last meeting I would attend for six and a half years.

Some people don't believe gambling to be a disease because there are no physical signs of it. *'It doesn't damage your heart and liver like alcohol does, nor does it cause brain damage like narcotics can.'*

This is a common misconception.

By the time I got home that night, I had genuine difficulty recalling the events of the previous eight hours. I doubted whether or not it even happened. I couldn't remember calling home earlier. I couldn't remember which bookies I had been in. And most worryingly, I had no recollection of driving home from the meeting. I wasn't drunk or taking drugs, but I could have very easily caused a serious accident, maybe even killed people. Why? Because I was totally out of control, the same way someone drunk or high would be.

I was in big trouble, in so many ways.

Since I'd left treatment in late 1991, Gamblers Anonymous had become a staple of my everyday diet. If I wasn't going to a meeting on any given day, I would be in contact with a member or my sponsor by phone. It provided me with a way to feel that I was normal, that my disease wasn't unique and that there were hundreds – actually, thousands – of others out there with the same affliction. I wasn't alone.

I can conservatively estimate that between late 1991 and early 2004, I attended at least 1,800 meetings. I travelled the country to attend different ones, and when abroad on business, I always made it my business to find a local meeting.

After attending the meeting on the night I slipped, my phone rang so solidly – morning, noon and night – that I considered changing my number. Recovery groups like AA, NA and GA are known as fellowships for a reason. Their members all look out for each other, no matter what. The members at my last meeting knew I was in trouble.

In the case of recovering addicts, the saying 'you can't kid a kidder' is especially true. I might have tried to tell them all that I was okay, but they knew I wasn't.

As the days passed, I became more and more reclusive. I took sick leave from work. I didn't want to be there. My mind just wouldn't focus on anything. Old feelings started to return. My old friends fear, paranoia and self-loathing came back to visit me at regular intervals. I was afraid to go outside. I knew that if I did, there was a very good chance I'd end up in the nearest betting shop.

Memories came flooding back. Being broke. Getting arrested. The holding-cell door banging. Court appearances. The reality of the situation at that time was very different. I still had a very good job, great friends, the trust of my family and savings in the bank. I hadn't broken any laws, pulled any strokes or committed any crimes. Yet, feelings of impending doom were cascading down upon me like torrential rain. I was suffocating, as if my head was underwater. I was crying for help, but there was nobody there to hear me. All of a sudden, it was 15 years ago, and I was living in mental squalor again. I was either too proud or too scared to do anything about it.

If a fellow member had come to me in the same state I was currently in, I would have known exactly what advice to give them. First of all, I would congratulate them on being brave enough to contact another member to share what was going on with them. I would then advise them to get to the next available meeting – maybe even two in the same day. I would advise them to relinquish control of their finances to someone they trusted until they felt strong enough again. I would remind them of the 'People, Places and Things' mantra that is so commonly used across fellowships.

People: Avoid people who are actively gambling, drinking or using. Stay close to people who are in a good place with their own recovery.

Places: Avoid places that will make you think about gambling, such as betting shops, casinos, racetracks etc. Go to places where you can help yourself, such as meetings and friends' houses.

Things: Avoid things that can help you to have a bet. Don't carry cash, don't buy newspapers with racing pages in them etc.

If only I could have taken a dose of my own medicine. I could have told you everything you needed to do for a successful recovery, but when it came to heeding my own advice, I just couldn't do it. It started with shame. I was mortified to have had to tell my sponsor and the meeting about my slip. I was an old-timer, and people throughout the national fellowship looked up to me and my recovery. How could I look at any of them straight in the face again?

The first of my fatal flaws had kicked in already. My ego. It had suffered a knockout blow from which it might never recover. I had given people within the fellowship cause to look at me sympathetically. It could never be the same again. That was the main reason I chose there and then to stop going to my meetings. It was a fatal decision, and one that would shape the next six years.

Every addict has at least one enabler when they are active in their addiction. I had three: both my parents and my boss. My parents loved me and tried to solve my problems by paying my debts. That was their way of enabling me. Bob's way was far more self-serving. I was the main cash cow at the office, the one who brought in the big deals. Bob knew this, and he lived a millionaire's lifestyle as a result of it. He enabled me – mainly because he greatly benefited from it. There was nothing I couldn't get away with: I worked when I wanted, I could pull contra deals with clients for free flights, tickets and more, and dupe clients into lending me money under stupid false pretences (like my car got broken into and my wallet was stolen). I knew he'd turn a blind eye to it all because I made him so much money.

The term 'enabler' generally describes someone whose behaviour allows a loved one to continue self-destructive patterns of behaviour.

This term can be stigmatising since there's often negative judgement attached to it. However, many people who enable others don't do so intentionally. They may not even realise they're doing it. This was true in the case of my parents.

Enabling usually refers to patterns that appear in the context of drug or alcohol misuse and addiction. However, enabling can describe any situation where you 'help' by attempting to hide problems or make them go away. In addition, according to the American Psychological Association, it can refer to patterns within close relationships that support any harmful or problematic behaviour and make it easier for that behaviour to continue. That was Bob's thing: exploitation through enabling.

Enabling doesn't mean you support your loved one's addiction or other behaviour. You might simply believe that, if you don't help, the outcome for everyone involved will be far worse. Maybe you excuse troubling behaviour, lend money or assist in other ways.

But it's important to realise that enabling doesn't really help, because it usually doesn't make a problem go away. It often makes it worse, since an enabled person has less motivation to make changes if they keep getting help that reduces their need to do so. It's difficult for someone to get help if they don't fully see the consequences of their actions.

It's not always easy to distinguish between empowering someone and enabling them. Most people who enable loved ones don't intend to cause harm. In fact, enabling generally begins with the desire to help. Enabling behaviours can often seem like helping behaviours. You may try to help with the best of intentions and enable someone without realising it.

Empowering someone doesn't mean solving or covering up problems. Rather, when you empower someone, you do one or more of the following to help them succeed or change on their own:

- Give them tools.
- Help them access resources.
- Teach them skills.

In other words, you give them the power to make their own choices and solve problems.

I have not gone to work now in over a week. I haven't been down home. The only place I've gone out to is the local Spar shop to stock up on food and other essentials. I've been ignoring all calls from GA people and pretending to have the flu when family or friends call. The phone rings again. The caller ID says, 'Bob G'.

'Hello there, my friend,' booms the loud voice down the line. 'How are you? We're all worried about you here; the place isn't the same without you.'

'I'm nearly better,' I mutter. 'I'll probably be back in on Monday.'

'That's the spirit,' he says. 'Advertising cures all illness. Get in here, get back in the groove, and you'll be back to normal in no time.'

I'm going to have to get back on the horse at some stage, and in a way he is right. Getting stuck into work and making money is probably a good way to help me get over my slip. After all, nobody died. It was a one-time thing. *I can do this,* I tell myself; *no problem.*

I jump in the shower, get dressed and pack a bag. I'm going to go home for a few days and be positive. A few beers with my dad and the lads will be nice, and it'll be good to see Mam again too.

There will be no gambling – not even a thought of it. I'm going to have a normal weekend. 'Normal' as in how weekends have been for the last 13 years.

On the drive back up on Sunday night, I mentally prepare myself for going back to work and try to devise a way to get this gambling monkey off my back. I know the only way to do it is to get to a meeting and talk to my sponsor. But my arch-enemy, pride, is standing in the way of that.

Anyway, I tell myself, *I have years of recovery behind me. I know better than anyone how to do this on my own.* And so, I decide. *Alone. That's how I'm going to do this.*

One of Sister Mairéad's famous phrases comes to mind. The 'stinking thinking' has returned. 'Stinking thinking' is a term to describe the state of mind of an active addict. It is, quite simply, what it says: having bad, polluted thoughts and ideas floating around in your head. In this instance, my thinking wasn't just stinking – it was reeking. I was filling up with arrogance and pride again.

CHAPTER 13

The World Health Organization officially recognises alcoholism as a disease. This means that if you are an alcoholic, your health insurance provider will cover any number of ailments that may develop as a result of your addiction. Liver disease, cancers, diabetes, cardiac problems and mental health issues are the primary afflictions linked to severe alcoholism. I believe it's only right that the WHO recognises this killer disease, and that those affected by it (who are lucky enough to have health insurance) are in a position to get the care they need. It also means that treatment centres can bill the insurance provider for the cost of treatment for an alcoholic.

I was in treatment in 2010. When I visited the administrator to discuss payment, I was quite amused to be told that if I was in rehab for alcoholism or drug addiction, my Vhi would cover the cost of my treatment. It was ironic then that I, a master schemer, would fill out my paperwork honestly and state that my reason for being in treatment was that I was a gambling addict. I had to pay the fees to the treatment centre out of my own pocket … and it took me years to do it.

My point here is that I am every bit as chronic an addict as the worst alcoholic or drug addict out there. But to this day, there is still a profound ignorance when it comes to gambling and its dangers. I always only refer to my own story when making statements about gambling, but I challenge anybody out there who may read this book to tell me at the end of it that I'm not a chronic addict. Yet the disease is not recognised as one, simply because there is no chemical dependence or obvious physical impact. I say no obvious physical impact, but for someone who was so active in my youth, I am now morbidly obese, suffer from anxiety and panic attacks, and more than one counsellor or doctor has indicated to me that they feel I am suffering from depression.

Then there's the financial element, and how it affects both the gambler and their family. In many cases, addiction isn't just about the addict – it's a family disease. When doing Step One in treatment, you are asked to write an honest inventory of how much your addiction has cost you.

Back in 2010, I did a very honest, searching inventory; after 25 years of gambling, I was able to account for almost €1 million. This figure (which would rise significantly five years later) was estimated from 20 years of a very good salary on top of the money I had stolen to feed my habit and winnings I had accrued along the way. If I were an alcoholic, I probably would drink a bottle of vodka and a few pints a day before passing out, and after a few years, I'd eventually die. If I was a drug addict, a few lines of whatever would be my drug of choice; the total cost of addiction would be around €500 a week. I have often lost that much on a 30-second greyhound race. That's the thing about a gambling addiction: it has no limits. You never get the highs someone addicted to a substance gets, and you never get enough of betting, win or lose. As long as they have enough in their pocket to place a bet, a compulsive gambler will keep betting.

And out of all of that money I accumulated, earned, stole, borrowed or won over the years, all I have to show for it is a half-decent wardrobe, a few memorable holidays or trips to matches and nothing else. And, of course, a criminal record.

CHAPTER 14

To those who knew me from home, such as my family and friends, everything seemed fine. My outer shell had not cracked, even though inside I was falling apart at a rate of knots. I still drove the fancy car home at weekends. I wore the Ralph Lauren shirts. I was still travelling to matches and taking nice holidays. To my friends, I remained The Man, and my folks were delighted that I was making something of myself and that the gardaí had stopped calling to the house.

Part of me was convinced I could control my gambling. That's the devious part of the addiction. I wasn't gambling every day, and the amounts weren't always big; sometimes I'd only bring €100 in with me and go home when I'd lost it. Some days I'd win €1,000. And I was happy with this behaviour because I thought I was controlling it. But I really wasn't. It had me just where it wanted me at that time.

Every two years, my friends and I would go on a rugby trip to Swansea for the Ireland v Wales Six Nations game. We would travel by bus and boat from Limerick. It was an epic journey that took 12 hours each way. It involved lots of drinking and general tomfoolery. We always eagerly looked forward to it, and it provided talking points for the pub at home for months afterwards. We would each carry £300 for the trip. This comfortably provided us with enough beer money and a little more for food and emergencies.

For the 2005 trip, I was under pressure at work, so I decided that I would drive myself, and we could all meet at the hotel. I took the ferry from Dublin and drove down from Holyhead – a four-hour drive. I decided to break up the journey and stopped in a town for coffee and a sandwich. After finishing my snack, I was walking back to my car when I happened upon a Coral bookmakers.

I looked at my watch and decided to go in for one bet. The first bet went well: a £50 stake on a horse that won at 2/1. This was followed by another winner, a greyhound at 5/2, the same £50 stake wagered. This immediately put me £275 in clover. Happy with my lot, and convincing myself that I could control things, I cashed out and made for my car.

I was back on the road, thinking that I would stand the lads a curry that night. We always went to a pub in Neath on the Thursday night for a meal. But the curry, and everything else, soon went out the window as my so-called self-control went up in smoke.

I was approaching the town centre, a few short miles from my final destination, when I saw another bookmakers, this time a William Hill. It was as if there was a magnetic force attached to the shop's sign that pulled me towards it. The next thing I knew, I was parked up and walking towards the front door. This time, I stopped to think. Not about whether or not I was going in (that was a foregone conclusion), but that this time I was the one in control.

I looked at the contents of my wallet. I took out the £275 winnings from the previous town and put it in my shirt pocket. I then closed my wallet, which contained my £300 spending money and around €250. I opened the glove compartment and locked the wallet in. As I closed the car door and walked towards the bookies, I felt good. I was in control. I had decided how much I was going to wager, and that demonstrated that my addiction hadn't gotten the better of me. I was beating it. And boy, it felt good.

My first bet was a £100 stake on a greyhound. He stumbled coming out of the traps. Game over. I quickly looked up at the screens and saw that there was a horse race off in one minute. With no time to study the form, a normal gambler would let the race go. Not me. I picked the second favourite because its odds were 3/1. I placed £75 on it, which would yield me a £300 return. The horse was tailed off in last place 60 seconds later.

I had £100 left. I was going to be smart about this. I found a race due off in ten minutes, so I would study the form and recoup my losses. A 7/4 favourite caught my eye. The fact that, if I placed the £100 on it, my return would be £275 (the exact amount I had walked in with a few minutes earlier) was also a contributing factor. I placed the bet.

It was a great race, the three market leaders battling it out in the final furlong. Unfortunately, for me, it wasn't that great. My horse was beaten by the narrowest of margins. It went to a photo finish. I knew my guy had been beaten, but I still clung to that docket like it was a winning lottery ticket for the next three minutes, until it was confirmed.

That was that. I had blown the £275 I had won in the space of 15 minutes. That was almost as much as we each had planned to spend over the entire weekend. I felt no remorse. Why would I? It was bonus money, money I had won. I still had everything I had left Dublin with earlier that afternoon in my wallet in the car. *No harm, no foul*, I thought.

I walked back to the car, sat in and buckled up. I checked the glove compartment for my wallet and took it out. My next move was not to drive on to Swansea. I put the wallet back in my pocket, got out of the car and went straight back through the door of the bookies.

Within 15 minutes, the £300 I had was gone, lost to two greyhounds and one very slow horse. There was a bureau de change next door. They changed the €250 to £210 for me. That lasted another 20 minutes. I walked back to the car, penniless. That old familiar numb feeling had come back.

I sat there thankful for one thing only: I had left my ATM and Visa cards at home. I didn't think I'd need them as I had plenty of cash. After a while, a text came through to my phone: *Just landed at the hotel. How far away are you?* The lads had arrived. Quickly, and almost as if it was second nature to me, I started to concoct a bullshit story. I was going to have to borrow cash from them, and I needed to save face.

I arrived at the hotel around a half-hour later. Thankfully, we all had prepaid for our accommodation months earlier. I walked into the bar and was met by a big welcoming shout from the lads, who were on their second or third beer. My story was short and sweet: some bastard had broken into my car while I was pulled in for a coffee. He helped himself to my wallet and laptop, and I was left with small change for the weekend.

Outrage ensued. Calls of 'fucking bastards, nothing's safe these days' were followed by 'hard luck, pal'. Without even asking, every one of them put their hands in their pockets and placed £50 in front of me. Thanks to them, I had a great weekend, and I soon forgot about my bout of madness on the way to Swansea. However, deep down inside, I felt sick. These guys were my best friends, and I had conned them.

Today, those guys are still my best friends. Why, I don't know. Sometimes I can't believe just how lucky I am.

CHAPTER 15

Today there is a slightly greater awareness of gambling being a problem. Gambling companies put fancy advertisements on television warning you to be 'Gamble Aware' and to never bet more than you can afford. They even provide helplines, should you feel the need to talk to someone. However, my opinion is that these advertisements are there to ease their consciences, and to provide proof to licensing authorities and governments that they care about the welfare of their customers. Bullshit!

To call gambling a 'game of chance' evokes fun, random luck and a sense of collective engagement. These playful connotations may be part of why almost 80 per cent of Irish adults gamble at some point in their lifetime. When I ask people without a gambling problem why they gamble, the most common answers are for pleasure, money or the thrill.

While these might be reasons for people to gamble initially, psychologists don't know why, for some, gambling stops being an enjoyable diversion and becomes compulsive. What keeps people playing even when it stops being fun? Why stick with games people know are designed for them to lose? Are some people just unluckier than others, or simply worse at calculating the odds?

As a chronic gambling addict for the past 35 years, I've tried my damn best to get to the root of why I ended up addicted. I've looked to the brain to understand the hooks that make gambling so compelling. I've found that many are intentionally hidden in the way gambling is marketed – it is designed to attract. These hooks work on casual casino goers, bingo players and those doing the lottery just as well as they do on problem gamblers.

One of the hallmarks of gambling is uncertainty – whether it's the size of a jackpot or the probability of winning at all. And reward uncertainty plays a crucial role in gambling's attraction.

Dopamine, the neurotransmitter the brain releases during enjoyable activities such as eating, sex and drugs, is also released during situations where the reward is uncertain. Dopamine release increases particularly in the moments leading up to a potential reward. This anticipation effect might explain why dopamine release parallels an individual's levels of gambling and the severity of their gambling addiction. It likely also plays a role in reinforcing the risk-taking behaviour seen in gambling.

Studies have shown that gambling triggers the same release of dopamine in the brain as taking a drug. Similar to drugs, repeated exposure to gambling and uncertainty produces lasting changes in the human brain. These reward pathways, similar to those seen in individuals suffering from drug addiction, become hypersensitive. Animal studies suggest that these brain changes due to uncertainty can even enhance gamblers' cravings and desire for addictive drugs.

Repeated exposure to gambling and uncertainty can even change how you respond to losing. Counter-intuitively, in individuals with a gambling problem, losing money comes to trigger the rewarding release of dopamine almost to the same degree that winning does. As a result, in problem gamblers, losing sets off the urge to keep playing, rather than the disappointment that might prompt you to walk away. This phenomenon is known as chasing losses.

But gambling is more than just winning and losing. It can be a whole immersive environment with an array of flashing lights and sounds. This is particularly true in a busy casino, but even a game or gambling app on a smartphone includes plenty of audio and visual frills to capture your attention.

But are they just frills? Studies suggest that these lights and sounds become more attractive and capable of triggering urges to gamble when they are paired with reward uncertainty. In particular, win-associated cues – such as jingles that vary in length as a function of jackpot size – increase excitement and lead gamblers to overestimate how often they are winning. Crucially, they can also keep you gambling longer and encourage you to play faster.

Since games of chance are set up so the house always has an advantage, a gambler wins infrequently at best. You might only rarely experience the lights and sounds that come along with hitting a true jackpot.

When you engage in recreational gambling, you are not simply playing against the odds, but also battling an enemy trained in the art of deceit and subterfuge. My particular vices are horse racing, greyhounds and sports betting. However, games of chance such as poker machines have a vested interest in hooking players for longer and letting them eventually walk away with the impression that they did better than chance, fostering a false impression of skill.

For many people, these carefully designed outcomes enhance the satisfaction they get from gambling. It may remain easy for them to simply walk away when the chips run out.

But gambling isn't only a light-hearted promise of a good time and a possible jackpot. For many every new day brings suffering from what's recently been reclassified as gambling disorder.

It stands out as one of the few addictions that doesn't involve the consumption of a substance, such as a drug or alcohol. Like other forms of addiction, though, gambling disorder is a solitary and isolating experience. It's tied to growing anxiety, and problem gamblers are, in my opinion, at greater risk of suicide.

For these more susceptible individuals, the hooks dangled by major betting companies and casinos start to seem more sinister. A solution to life's problems always feels just one bet away.

It never is.

CHAPTER 16

It was alarming to look at my bank account online during this time. I had a decent five-figure sum saved over the years, one that would have easily sorted out a deposit on a nice house. But now that I was gambling again, the nest egg had started to disappear, and in a very rapid fashion, too.

I wasn't getting into any trouble. This was largely because I had a steady source of good income, and the savings as backup. I didn't need to scheme and pull strokes as I had plenty of fluid cash available to me. On the plus side for Bob, my return to gambling meant that, as somebody who earned large commissions on big sales orders, I was working twice as hard as usual. My sales figures had gone through the roof, and my pay cheques every Friday were substantial.

I had, however, started to take earlier lunch breaks and return later in the afternoon. This was so I could get at least two good-quality hours in the bookies. It didn't go unnoticed by Bob, but he was prepared to allow me as much leeway as I wanted provided my weekly sales report was much better than expected. It also didn't go unnoticed by others in the office. I wasn't fooling anybody but myself.

One of the many and most dangerous character flaws a compulsive gambler has is pride. I am no different. Pride was in many ways my downfall, as the saying goes.

I lived in Dublin for 21 years. What nobody close to me knew was that for certain periods of that time, I was homeless. Not my family, not my close friends, or my colleagues. Not a single soul on earth, but me. To the majority, homelessness is characterised by some scruffy, unkempt poor soul who is asleep in a doorway, covered by a tatty blanket with a begging bowl in front of them. I never got to that stage, but only by the grace of God.

I was first evicted from an apartment I was renting in 2007. Ironically, I was renting it from a garda. It was a lovely flat in Castleknock. I was devastated to lose it, but the gambling was so out of control at this stage, I couldn't maintain it. Once I had stopped deluding myself that I could control the gambling and it spiralled, I blew through my savings in a couple of months and was back to the seedy world of living hand to mouth and pulling small scams.

The very idea that a man as successful as I was in my professional life could be homeless is beyond comprehension. I always had plenty of cash to splash around at the weekend or for trips away and nice clothes. To those in my social circle, I was a success story, the guy who had it all: the big job, lots of travel, the BMW 5 Series, the Italian suits. All status symbols that enabled me greatly in my addiction, as they were props for the various scams that I perpetuated to get by.

But the reality of it was that, while in the throes of addiction, I spent every last cent that I earned, borrowed or stole in the bookies. I stopped buying nice clothes, going on holidays and attending sporting events. I was having to leave my driver's licence or passport at petrol stations as collateral for fuel I wasn't able to pay for. My grandmother used a common phrase – 'real fur coat, no knickers' – to describe the type of person I had become: all style on the outside but emotionally, morally and financially bankrupt inside.

I was constantly being evicted from apartments because of my inability to pay the rent. I was a drifter, going from one destination to the other, almost in a trance. In between apartments, I would stay in hotels and bed and breakfasts, often coming up with a way of not paying. Then, I'd find an apartment in *The Herald* and pretend to an unassuming landlord that I'd transferred the deposit and rent through the bank. Back then, a bank transfer could take up to five working days, so I'd use my charm, get the keys and have my foot in the door. After that, I either had time to sort out the rent or I would prolong the lie with the landlord. But eventually, the hens would come home to roost, and I'd be out on my ear, searching for a bed for the night somewhere else.

I would often stay in hotels when between apartments. I did this for a variety of reasons. Firstly, I enjoyed the comfort and security. Secondly, hotels were often easier to cheat and more likely not to detect they were being scammed or put on the long finger for payment. This suited me fine, and it worked very well. When I couldn't afford to pay, the majority would fall for the 'money has been transferred' line or seek payment from my job. I was, after all, wearing Armani and driving a flashy 5 Series. And almost all did get paid eventually (my way of justifying everything to my deluded self).

On one occasion, my hotel scam nearly cost me my life. There was a nice big hotel with a leisure centre on the outskirts of Dublin. I booked in on a Monday evening for four nights. The usual story applied: the money had been transferred by the company and would be with them the following day. When it wasn't, I apologetically told them that it would definitely be there the next day, which they seemed to accept. Or so I thought.

When the money wasn't there on the Wednesday, an attractive, well-dressed lady came to me as I was eating my dinner and told me that the manager would like to say hello to me. She said that he was impressed with what I did for a living and wanted to explore the possibility of us doing further business. The dollar signs started ringing in my head, and I went with her up one flight of stairs and into what seemed to be an office. Big mistake!

When I entered the room, I found that it wasn't an office, but a mini conference room. It was a large empty space, only for one chair placed in the centre of the room. I was greeted by four thugs – that's the only way to describe them. The leader of the group was a tanned, stocky, dark-haired guy, foreign, maybe Italian, maybe Eastern European. He smiled at me, told me to take a seat and proceeded to take a mini sledgehammer from inside his jacket. He told me that I had one hour to get him his money, or else! The implication was clear.

What really shocked me was the attractive, well-dressed 'lady'. She stood at the shoulder of the ringleader with a sinister smile on her face, all the while pleading with him to let her 'take a few swings at the prick'. I knew I was in really deep trouble. I had only €60 on me and was facing a €400 bill. I could feel my legs shake. It's a good job I was sitting down because I was so scared there was no way my legs would have supported me. They locked me in the room and left.

I spent the next hour trying to come up with a way to appease them, but my silver-tongued bullshit wasn't going to get me out of this one. I had no choice but to fall back on my get-out-of-jail card. When they came back, I gave them Bob's number, telling them he was my boss and that he'd probably sort it out. They left the room again.

What seemed like an eternity passed, and then the door swung open again. I was told to get up and get out. The jelly-like feeling in my legs was still there, and I couldn't stand up. It took me about five minutes to compose myself. My bag containing my belongings was waiting for me at the door, and I was escorted downstairs. Bob was standing at the reception desk with his trusted sidekick. They were smiling and joking with the attractive 'lady'. He looked at me in the way a disappointed teacher would at his star pupil, and he told me he'd see me in the morning. I knew there'd be hell to pay then, but at least I was getting out of there alive. When I got to my car, I noticed that a six-inch nail had been driven into my front driver's-side tyre. A goodbye gift. I changed the tyre and got the hell out of there.

I found a B&B nearby advertising rooms for €40. I gladly availed of it. I went to sleep that night thinking of what might have been. But, to give you an indication of how sick my mind was at the time, I was pissed off that now there was another big favour I owed Bob, and that he'd take the €400 out of my wages. No gratitude towards him for probably saving me from getting killed. I found out subsequently that the hotel was a front for some very serious gangland criminals. To this day I probably don't realise fully how close I came to becoming another gangland statistic.

Looking back, it was a truly horrific existence. I say 'existence' because that's all I was doing at that time – existing. I certainly wasn't living, that's for sure. But that's what gambling did to me. It stripped me bare of any semblance of self-worth. I hated myself from the minute I woke in the morning to the minute my head hit whatever pillow I was lucky enough to be laying it on at night. But despite the self-loathing, I could still see only positives in my future, and those positives would be fuelled by the prospect of that big win, the one in which I would take the bookie to the cleaners for tens of thousands, enough to set me up for life.

I was back living in Walter Mitty land, only this time it was far more delusional than it had been 20-odd years ago when I had first moved there. And there was nothing I could do to help myself. My pride simply wouldn't let me.

CHAPTER 17

t was now approaching Christmas 2007. Life at this time was probably as unmanageable as it ever had been. The gambling was constant. Every day, at lunchtime and straight after work. And the lunch breaks were getting longer, the finishing times earlier.

I was using a dating site around this time and going on a lot of dates, both in Dublin and at home in Limerick. I really did have a desire to settle down. I was approaching 40 and believed that being in a long-term, steady relationship or married would put me back on the straight and narrow. I had convinced myself that there was no way I'd risk screwing up the right relationship when it came along. The time was right for me to try and meet Miss Right.

I met a girl in Limerick around this time. We'll call her Sandra. We met for a drink, had a really good night where we talked and laughed a lot, and decided that we'd try it again. So we did. We then embarked on a two-and-a-half-year merry-go-round of a relationship where I dug so many deep holes for myself that I was amazed I didn't reach Australia.

Initially, it was great. Sandra introduced me to her family right away, and we all seemed to hit it off. But my insecurities kicked in almost immediately, and I felt that I wasn't good enough for them. My instinct in these matters is to put on a mask, pretend I'm something I'm not and impress the hell out of them. So I did. I took Sandra away on lavish weekend breaks and holidays; we visited New York, London (several times), Croatia, Berlin and Paris. She loved the trips (who wouldn't?), and just as important to me, her family were impressed.

I even sent her mother on a few trips with her. I was The Man, and I loved it all.

What none of them knew was how I financed all of those trips. They were all paid for by big gambling wins, or by deception. I had scammed two prominent travel agents into providing me with lines of credit that I could never repay. Both saw fit to have me arrested and charged with the crimes. I received suspended sentences for both, after repaying them. I managed to keep this a secret from Sandra and her family. How, I'm not sure, but I did.

After two years, the relationship was starting to fade. It had become more and more obvious to me that there was no real attraction left, for either of us. Sandra had wanted desperately to become pregnant but couldn't. This caused a lot of friction. Also at this time, one of her brothers and her younger sister found out about my past and told her everything. The relationship ended with a bang one Sunday when Sandra came home after a night out with her sister. She came through the door drunk and argumentative, and everything came out: the trust issues and, most importantly, my inability to provide her with a child. The trust issues were enough on their own; sadly, her inability to have children was down to complications she had suffered in a miscarriage many years previously. I understood her anger and frustration. She too was nearing the 40 mark and was desperate to start a family. She had put all her chips on me, and it hadn't worked. She started throwing plates and cups, so I went upstairs, packed my bag and drove to Dublin at 4 a.m.

We never spoke again.

It was around this time that I pulled a stroke that would be the straw that broke the camel's back. It would be the closest I had come to a lengthy prison sentence, and it also put my face in the national press.

Bob, my boss, was involved in a multimillion-euro property deal. He liked to boast about it, and we had many long chats where he would tell me his plans and keep me up to speed with what was happening. He was using a new bank for the finance and regularly cited the assistant manager's name during our discussions. One day, I decided to use this knowledge to my advantage.

I called the bank and asked to speak to Bob's contact. I introduced myself as Bob's sales manager and asked if I could come to see him since I was selling a property in the UK and wanted to invest the proceeds. All of this was complete bullshit, of course, but given the magnitude of his dealings with Bob, and the fact that I worked for him, he was delighted to help me.

At our first meeting, I brought my passport, utility bill and pay slip, and I opened an account. All perfectly above board and legal. A couple of days later, my ATM card arrived, and the account was open. I followed this up by calling the bank manager and informing him that the sale of my UK property had been processed and that the money would arrive in a couple of weeks. I then mentioned that I might need a temporary overdraft – nothing major – to tide me over until the funds came in. There and then, he put an initial €1,500 overdraft limit on the account. Happy days. I couldn't believe how easy it had been. Then the greed associated with compulsive gambling kicked in.

Over the next two weeks, I requested extensions to the overdraft. Before I knew it, I had exceeded the €10,500 mark. This obviously startled somebody in the bank, and my account was flagged. Game over. But my arrogance told me to just lie low. They'd chase me for a few months, soon get sick of me and eventually forget about it. I also knew they couldn't tell Bob because of client confidentiality. My arrogance, not for the first or last time, was very, very misplaced.

One day I received a call at work from the gardaí at Store Street Garda Station. The detective said she needed to speak to me, and that it'd be less embarrassing for me if I came in voluntarily. I went to the station the next morning, and I was arrested at the front desk. When interviewed, I did what I had always done: admitted everything and got it over with as soon as I could.

A few weeks later, I was charged with theft by deception and told to appear in court. But this time, the game had changed: because of the amount of money involved, I was to be tried in the Circuit Court. This meant that I would be looking at a far greater sentence. The reality of what I had done, and the seriousness of the matter, finally started to permeate my thick skull. I was in deep shit this time, for sure.

The fallout from this was bad. I appeared in court on a Friday morning in February 2009. As per usual, I told nobody, thinking this was going to be another thing I could sweep under the carpet and deal with down the road. The following Monday morning, when I got to the office, my secretary told me that I had missed several calls from my dad. I looked at my mobile, which was on silent, and saw a barrage of missed calls and texts, not only from my dad and from my friends, but my sister (the one who was on speaking terms with me). Something was up.

I locked the door to my office and asked not to be disturbed. My first call was to one of my friends. He broke it to me: my arrest and charge had been plastered all over the local media, both newspaper and radio. I felt nauseous. Personally, I could take the hit – I had had it coming, after all – but I knew that this would destroy my family. I made the call home and got it with both barrels. And I deserved it, every single bit of it. I was only too relieved to be miles away from home then, in Dublin.

There was a lot of tension at home for the next few weeks and months. My friends, although they never shunned me, were also disgusted at how I had let my life get to this stage. I started going to Gamblers Anonymous meetings again, and I also started seeing a counsellor. But truth be told, I was doing these things only to start to develop a prettier picture of myself for the judge, one that would hopefully garner sympathy. Because whatever sentence I would get at the end of this court case would be significant. And there would be no immediate appeal to see me out on bail.

But there was one thing that didn't change throughout all of this – I was still gambling. And more recklessly and frequently than ever. I was still infatuated with the notion of the 'big win', the one that would cure all ills, my own personal panacea.

CHAPTER 18

t's 7 p.m. on a mundane Tuesday night. Johnny puts down his cup of tea for a minute and reaches for the remote control. Ah, sure, Tuesdays are boring, but wait … there's a half-decent Champions League game on RTÉ: Juventus v some other team from an unpronounceable part of Europe that's been recently formed. *Home and Away* is just over, and Johnny's waiting for the game to start. If only the game was on BBC … no bloody ads!

The annoying Go Compare and Barry's Tea ads are over … surely not many more now. Then, the Paddy Power ad comes on. It's quite humorous. Johnny has been following the Paddy Power ads – initially, because of the humour, though lately he's becoming attracted to what they offer. It's offering him €50 in free bets for no reason other than to become a new customer tonight. And it's only a tenner to join. 'Not for me, I'll pass,' says Johnny.

The game's about to kick off. Ronaldo is playing. Johnny tells himself, *If I had signed up to Paddy Power's very generous offer, I would have bet €10 on Ronaldo scoring the first goal. 4/1 odds … that means I'd have won €40 and got my tenner back if he scored first. And I'd also have the €50 in free bets from the sign-up offer. But really, what are the chances of Ronaldo scoring first? There are 22 players on the field, so why is he only 4/1? Gambling is for mugs … they aren't catching me.*

Twenty-five minutes go by. It's a poor game. *Ha ha, Paddy Power, you didn't dupe me,* Johnny's telling himself. Then, the Juventus winger is clean through. Only the keeper to beat. He must score. The keeper trips him up. Penalty. Up steps Ronaldo, ball in hand. 'Miss it, miss it,' Johnny silently mutters under his breath. Does he miss it? The hell he does. All of a sudden, Johnny's consumed with rage, anger and adrenaline. His mind is racing. *I should be up €40 now and have €50 in free bets.*

Half-time comes. Time for another cuppa. Just as Johnny gets up, there's another ad from Paddy Power offering 8/1 on Ronaldo scoring a hat-trick. *I'm not missing out again*, he tells himself. He grabs his phone and downloads the app. Debit card details entered, and he's made his first deposit. All done in five minutes. *I'm in business now!* Johnny places the bet, sits back and waits for his winnings to appear.

It's now 10 p.m. Johnny's out the back, in the shed. Hiding from the wife in case she sees his excessive use of the phone. Ronaldo was substituted after 60 minutes. No hat-trick. The €50 in free bets failed to find Johnny a winner, as did the other €30 he deposited during the game. Now, he's thinking about how he's going to explain the name Paddy Power on the joint account.

The picture I have just painted is not fiction. It's happening every hour of every day across the country and abroad. When I was a kid growing up in the 1970s and '80s, gambling was backing a horse. And even doing that was difficult. You had to go into a betting shop. There was an element of shame to that that kept a lot of men out of the bookies. Today, you can gamble to your heart's content, 24 hours a day, totally undetected. All you need is a smartphone and a prepaid credit card. Technology has evolved in the most wonderful of ways. It has created scientific, medical and engineering miracles. It has also created a new addiction, one far more potent and destructive in many ways than alcohol or drugs. Gambling is the fastest-growing reason people are in treatment centres and prisons today. And it's technology that has made it so.

I don't mean to sound like a killjoy. Having a flutter, or a night at the dogs, can be a great pastime. Unfortunately, for a growing number of people, it is certainly no pastime. Back in those early days, you would bet on horses or greyhounds. Nothing more. Log on to the Paddy Power website, or that of any of its competitors, and you will be encouraged to have a bet on football, rugby, tennis, golf or *any* sport that is played, wherever in the world it is played. It doesn't stop there. To attract the ladies, you can bet on the lotto. There's even online bingo, with specific adverts on TV targeting pensioners to play at home rather than go to the bingo hall.

Look at the value of Flutter plc on the stock market. Sadly, a huge chunk of that success is down to people who become addicted to gambling, and that's caused in no small way by the ruthless, relentless advertising campaigns launched by these companies.

I know that there are people who don't think that gambling is an addiction because there are no apparent physical consequences as there are with alcoholism or drug addiction. Alcohol and drugs have ruined, and continue to ruin, countless lives every day in this country. Bear this in mind, though: you cannot drink alcohol or abuse drugs without people noticing. But you can gamble while sharing a meal, or being at the cinema, with your wife and kids, and they will never know. That is, not until you get sacked from your job for stealing; not until the bank sends out the bailiffs to repossess your home because of failed mortgage payments; or not until you continually disappoint your kids and deprive them of basics like proper food and education. And why? Because you've given everything to Mr Power.

The government banned cigarette advertising in the 1990s because it was promoting something that kills. Look at the ever-increasing suicide rate in this country, and I guarantee you there's a growing number of compulsive gamblers in there. Maybe it's time to follow suit and ban the promotion of this killer disease.

CHAPTER 19

B y July 2010, the heat was off, in the sense that people seemed to have forgotten about the media exposure, and I could go home at weekends and find things were back to normal. But they weren't. Far from it.

My gambling had hit an all-time high. I was hardly turning up for work at all. The relationship I had been in was finished. I was consumed by paranoia and fear. I wasn't living. I was merely existing. Something had to be done, so I decided to turn the clock back 19 years. I took a drive out to Bushy Park Treatment Centre and had an interview with the head of treatment, an absolute saint of a man called Frank Hunt. This was the first step on a long journey, but a very important one.

After my assessment (which I passed with flying colours), Frank called me the next day and told me to have a bag packed and be ready to be admitted within the next fortnight. This killed me. I didn't want to do this for a variety of reasons, the main one being shame, but also because it would interfere with my gambling. However, if I wanted to impress yet another judge, I needed to do this, because the charge I was facing was by far the most serious I had ever faced. My life depended upon it.

I awoke on the morning of 25 July (my parents' wedding anniversary) and faced my demons. I had spent the previous week plotting and scheming as to how I was going to make the next four weeks work best for me. I said my goodbyes at home, jumped in the car and drove the 40 minutes to Bushy Park Treatment Centre.

Upon arrival, the receptionist told me to wait in the hallway until Frank came to admit me. I was struck by how little the place had changed in 19 years. I was also struck by the beauty and character of the house and grounds. In the summertime, it is a glorious setting, and there is an incredible pathway through a wooded area at the rear of the house. Many a contemplative walk would be taken there over the next month.

After a short while, Frank came out. He put me at ease straight away. You couldn't help but be put at ease by Frank's manner. A recovering alcoholic himself, he fully understood every little facet of addiction and the damage it brings to both addicts and their families. He said one rather poignant thing to me as he was showing me to my room.

'You're here now, and regardless of the reason you're here, my advice to you is to make the most of it. Very few come in here because they want to. They come in because they need to, be it to appease a family member, to repair a family, to impress a judge or to save a job. It doesn't matter. What matters now is what you make of it.'

I could feel a bond forming with Frank there and then, and to this day I have nothing but the highest admiration for him.

After dinner, I was plunged straight into my first group therapy session. When that was finished, I mingled with the residents, introducing myself to them. Just like 19 years previously, there was an eclectic mix, and I started to process who I would affiliate myself with and who I would keep my distance from. In environments like those that exist in rehabilitation centres, there is always conflict between residents, and the core group usually splinters. This was no different, and I found myself gravitating towards a group of guys approximately my age, and deliberately avoiding a 'gang of four' who were younger and ... let's just say that they had a different perspective on life than I had.

On my first Sunday morning, I had to attend an AA meeting. This was a compulsory part of treatment, so I went along even though I wasn't an alcoholic. It was an open meeting, which meant that the public could attend, and from what I can remember, it was attended mostly by ex-residents. It was at this meeting that my recovery got real, as I met a blast from the past there, and my whole attitude and outlook changed as a result of it.

The residents were always first into a meeting. As tradition had it, we all huddled together in the back corner of the Portakabin where the meetings took place. The meeting started at 10.45 a.m. and lasted until midday. It was well attended, with approximately 25 recovering alcoholics in attendance, as well as us 12 residents.

Confidentiality is a big thing at these meetings, so I won't divulge much. I was a compulsive gambler and not an alcoholic, so I felt like a fish out of water with the stories being shared by those in attendance. None of my war stories seemed to match theirs. The alcoholic or drug addict suffers mostly physically. They have experiences that usually involve self-harm, domestic violence and blackouts. The life of an active compulsive gambler is one of secrecy and deceit, a hectic, frenetic lifestyle. One story did, however, shake me out of my bored slumber. I heard a woman speak in a distinctive accent. I couldn't quite put my finger on it, but she sounded familiar. I was afraid to look up, afraid of who I might see. Then, she addressed me in front of the whole group and proceeded to tell a story of how, 19 years ago, in this very house, both she and I had regularly locked horns, including one memorable fight over who controlled the TV remote in the house. My old sparring partner Nora!

As a gambler, I would have put my house, and yours, on Nora

falling into a dark hole very shortly after we came out of treatment in 1991 and drinking herself to death. Of all the people I got to know back then, she was on the top of my list not to make it. Now here she was, 19 years later, looking even younger than she had back then, full of life and not having touched a drop of alcohol since. I couldn't believe it. After the meeting, we had a good chat, and she hugged me and wished me well. It was an incredible experience. I had just met living proof that the 12-Step recovery programme works if you want it to. I was as proud of Nora as I had ever been of anyone in my life, and she provided me with huge inspiration there and then to finally grow up, take responsibility for my actions and make something of my life. Nora was still working the programme and attending AA meetings, even back in the place where she had done her treatment 19 years previously.

I thought about little else that day other than the time I had spent in this house with Nora and the others. I wondered where they all were now. Statistically, three out of every group of 12 make it in recovery. Not great odds. I knew that some of the others had gone to meet their Maker far earlier than they should have.

I met my designated counsellors the next day. For some reason, Frank had assigned two counsellors to me, whereas most of the rest of the group only had the one. Maybe I was double the trouble? My introduction to Gerry was great. He was softly spoken, considerate and caring. Very much the 'good cop' in the double act.

Then there was Pat. Talk about getting off on the wrong foot.

I was in the coffee room, in the middle of telling a joke to a captivated audience of four or five other residents. It was a funny joke, I could tell it well, and it was met with uproarious laughter. I turned around, and at the door stood a diminutive lady, late 50s, I reckoned.

I marked her down as a looker in her youth, but at this moment, she resembled a bulldog chewing a wasp.

'What's so funny?' she barked at me.

I was taken aback by this – I really wasn't impressed by her tone. And being full of arrogance and self-importance (and wanting to be the class joker), I told her so.

'Excuse me?' I said in reply, feigning hurt and indignance.

'Do you have hearing difficulties?' she asked.

'Actually, I don't. I don't know who you are, but to be honest with you, I don't appreciate your tone. It's quite rude to speak to people in that manner.'

I was feeling pleased with myself, having laid down a marker to one and all that I wouldn't be treated like that.

'This is a treatment centre,' she said. 'A very serious place. Keep your jokes to yourself, and perhaps take a long, hard look at why you're here.'

She turned on her heel and walked away. I was gobsmacked. Just who the hell did this woman think she was? The room went quiet, eerily quiet. It felt like I was six years old again, and the teacher had just admonished me in front of my classmates. I felt two feet tall and wanted to crawl under a rock somewhere.

After around five minutes I had composed myself and decided to up the ante. I wasn't going to let her get away with this. No way. I got up and headed for the office where I had watched her disappear five minutes earlier. I knocked on the door and was told to enter. When I did, she was reading a file. I decided that attack would be the best form of defence here.

'I don't know who you are, and I don't really care,' I said with great indignation. 'Nobody should speak to anyone in that manner, no matter what, and I'd like an apology.'

She remained silent, reading her file. She did this for about a minute, although it seemed longer. She then put the file down, spun around in the chair and looked at me.

'What can I do for you?' she asked.

I just stood there. For once in my life, I was stuck for words.

'Did you not hear what I just said?' I asked, having regained my composure.

'I heard some incoherent rambling alright, but I didn't pay any attention to it.'

I really couldn't believe the temerity of this woman.

'Forget it,' I said and made my way towards the door. I expected her to call me back, but instead, she just picked up the file she had been reading and started flicking through it again. As I reached the door, it opened, and Frank, the treatment manager, came in.

'Ah, Pat,' he said in his jolly tone. 'I see you've met Patricia, your second counsellor. I just know you're going to get along like a house on fire.'

My first instinct was to go up to my room, pack my bag and go home. There was no way that I could work with this bitch. Actually, there was no way I *would* work with her. I had my pride. I calmed down and went outside to catch some fresh air. I decided to walk around the forest. Halfway around there's a little bench where residents can sit and ponder. It's an idyllic little spot, and I was delighted to see that there was nobody there when I arrived. I sat down, full of anger and self-righteousness.

After ten minutes or so, I heard approaching footsteps, and I presumed it was one of the residents, probably in a similar headspace to myself.

'Can I join you?' was the question. A woman's voice. I turned my head to see which resident it was, and standing there was Patricia, the she-devil.

'It's a free country,' I replied.

So, she sat with me. And we talked. She asked me why I felt the need to be the centre of attention. I was taken aback by this. I asked her what she meant, and she told me that that had been her first impression of me. She described the incident in the coffee room, and her view was that she could hear me before she could see me and that I was intent on entertaining and regaling the other residents. When I thought about it, she was bang on the money. My desire for popularity and to be accepted was there again, in abundance.

She asked me to describe what had led me back here after a 19-year hiatus. I started to tell her and found myself opening up to her. She just sat and listened. She was able to deduce from what I was telling her that I wasn't being entirely truthful, with either her or myself. She stood up, put her hand on my shoulder and said to me, 'We have a lot of work ahead of us … a lot of work.' Then she left me to my thoughts.

My thoughts were firstly to come up with ways to manipulate those around me, both staff and fellow residents, to make sure this would be an easy ride. After all, I had spent time here before, I was an old hand at this recovery business, and I could play the game better than anyone. But then my mind started to think back to the AA meeting and Nora. She really impressed me. I couldn't believe the changes in her. She looked fantastic, despite being 19 years older, and she looked so at peace with everything. When we first crossed paths, you could tell that she was an attractive woman, but she had suffered both the physical and mental effects of her alcoholism. She had been wild-eyed, hyperactive and a nervous wreck. Now she looked a million dollars, and the whole world could come crashing down around her and it wouldn't upset her. And she achieved all of this by living her life the way she'd learned to in this house.

I started to walk back towards the house and decided the same thing I had decided 19 years previously. I was going to try and make the most of this opportunity. It couldn't hurt. And maybe, just maybe, one day I'd have the kind of serenity that Nora had.

CHAPTER 20

n the first couple of weeks of treatment, Patricia lived up to her reputation as a ball-breaker. And mine were getting regularly smashed. There were five counsellors in the house, and Frank, the head of treatment, made six. Of those six, five were recovering addicts themselves. This provides great insight and empathy, and it goes a long way towards making a resident feel comfortable with their counsellor. Being the lucky guy I was, I drew the short straw there, too. Patricia was not a recovering addict, but she was married to one. She based a lot of her counselling methods on making the residents look at the damage they were doing to their families and the people who loved them.

Wednesday was still family day, and still by far the most dreaded day of the week for every resident. I was no different. For my first Wednesday session, my family members attending were my mother and younger sister. And, boy, were they prepped in how to go about this by Patricia. They destroyed me, and as before, I wasn't allowed to respond. I had to just sit there and listen. My mother spoke about the shame she felt every time she saw the neighbours gossiping after a police car had pulled up outside our house, and how she felt when she had to go into a pawnbroker to buy back her wedding ring. And this was in front of the whole group, and their family members, too. The Thursday morning group session was always hell because we picked the meatiest bones out of each other's character assassinations from the day before and confronted each other about them. It was rough, and tempers were often frayed. The little cliques would take each other's side, and this often led to needless arguments. And a lot of these arguments were fuelled by the counsellors.

Patricia – or Pat, as we now all called her – finally broke me after two weeks. I argued every conceivable point with her up to that stage, thinking that I was smarter than her. The reality of the situation was that she had eaten far worse cases than me for breakfast and spat out the bad bits. One morning, I was preparing for a group session she was leading, and no matter how hard I tried, I couldn't muster up the strength or the logic to argue with her anymore. I didn't participate at all in that group session. I just sat there and listened. I didn't offer feedback to every point made by a fellow resident; I didn't force my opinion down everybody's throats. I just listened. And learned. At the end of the session, Pat asked me to stay behind for a minute. She said nothing for a while, then asked me how I was. I told her that I was good, in every way. My head was clearer. She smiled at me and told me that there was hope for me yet. I was proud as a peacock.

I spoke very fondly earlier about Sister Mairéad, the lady who founded the treatment centre back in 1991. To this day I speak of Patricia with the same affection. I learned so much from her in my time in the house and afterwards, but the most important gift she gave me was the ability to love myself again. She taught me the importance of listening to others, why it's not always important to be heard all the time and that, in order to get better, I was going to have to drop the act, take off the many different masks I had been wearing and concentrate on myself.

The final two weeks of treatment flew. And they were both extremely enjoyable and excruciatingly painful. I chose Pat to read my Step Five with. This is where you unburden yourself of any secrets and things you are unduly ashamed of to one person. It's a confession of sorts. I chose Pat because I felt that, no matter what I told her, I wouldn't be judged. And I wasn't.

There was a beautiful little chapel on the grounds. It wasn't there back in '91, and it really added character, as well as providing a sanctuary if you needed to be alone. I chose the chapel as the spot to meet with Pat and do my Step Five. I had spent well over a week writing my Step Four, which is where you reflect and write what you need to say in your Step Five. I had well in excess of 40 pages written, and it was very comprehensive. We started the process, and I began to read it out.

I was halfway through the first page when Pat stood up, walked over to me and took the pages from me.

'I want you to tell me everything from your heart, not your head,' she said.

I was a bit peeved at this initially. I had spent a lot of time writing those pages and had been looking forward to reading them out.

'I'm not interested in your beautifully written descriptions,' she continued. 'What I want is for you to tell me everything, and to describe how you *feel*, not how you want to appear. This isn't a Hollywood script. This is your entire life, and this is your chance to take a huge leap forward. Talk to me.'

And talk to her I did. We entered that chapel at 1.30 p.m., just after dinner, and didn't come out until 5 p.m. Once I started talking, you couldn't shut me up. I told her my deepest, innermost secrets. Things that I have not told another soul to this very day. Things that I was very ashamed of. And she didn't flinch at any of them. There was no need for a conversation afterwards. There were tears aplenty on both sides. In the space of a month, I had gone from intensely disliking this woman to loving her in the way a child loves his mother. Pat made me feel safe. She made me feel wanted and, most of all, she made me love myself again.

I left treatment at the end of August. It was a Thursday afternoon and a glorious afternoon at that. My sister collected me, and she had some business in Kilkee, so I went along for the spin. The west coast of Clare is idyllic, especially when the sun is splitting the rocks. She went about her business, and I took a stroll on the beach and around the town. I was very positive mentally, but I still had my sentencing in the Circuit Court to look forward to. It was still the dominant thought in my mind, and it would be until my day in court: 8 November 2010.

I got home that evening around six o'clock. I had something to eat with my folks, then I jumped in the car. There was a Gamblers Anonymous meeting in Bushy Park at eight. I had undertaken to go to this meeting every week for a minimum of two years unless there were unforeseen circumstances. I intended to honour this commitment, so a mere seven hours after my discharge from the house, I found myself driving up the narrow road towards the Portakabin. It felt good, and I felt as though I belonged there. That was where I needed to be at that time.

CHAPTER 21

From the day of my discharge, my life had a new pattern. I agreed to cut down on my workload. I decided I was only going to work three days a week. Bob could take that or leave it. I had made that decision and, going forward, I was going to be making more and more decisions on my own. Decisions that would benefit me.

I would work on Wednesdays, Thursdays and Fridays. That way I was only going to be away from home two nights a week. I made a deal with a hotel near the office and got a very good rate, which I paid a month in advance. My life was dominated by my recovery, and I had a very set routine. On Mondays, I would meet some other guys in recovery for lunch, then go to my aftercare on Monday nights in the Pastoral Centre. On Tuesdays, I would drive to Ennis and go to a lunchtime meeting, and then for coffee with some other members in recovery. I would drive to Dublin early on Wednesdays, go to work, check into my accommodation and go to a GA meeting that night. Thursdays would be the same as Wednesdays, and after work on Fridays, I'd drive home, go to the local GA meeting and get home by ten o'clock. Saturdays would be spent with my parents, taking Mam shopping and then going to the pub with Dad. Later in the evening, I'd catch up with my friends, and we'd have a night out on the town. Sunday mornings were spent in Ennis, and a late breakfast in Café Aroma after a meeting at Bushy Park Treatment Centre. Sunday evenings were spent playing pool and darts with the lads.

I felt I had a good work–life–recovery balance, and I was starting to enjoy life. But I still had an albatross dangling from around my neck: my court sentencing, and 8 November was looming. The court case still consumed me. It was ever-present in my hourly thoughts. I had received an abundance of praise and encouragement from people, but in my mind, I was already done for.

The morning of 8 November 2010 was cold and murky in Limerick City. I was up at 6 a.m. My dad was coming to court with me. He was more tense and nervous than I was. The last few years had taken a significant toll on him. We had grown a lot closer over the past decade. He came on rugby trips with my friends and me, and we went to a lot of games. The one real thing we both shared was a passion for sport. We both loved the same teams: Manchester United, Munster Rugby and Shannon RFC. The only rivalry we had was Clare v Limerick in the hurling, but that was a friendly rivalry. He had become my friend as well as my dad. I know deep down he blamed himself for a lot of my shortcomings. If everything worked out today, I was determined that I'd never put him in this position again.

We got the 7.20 a.m. train to Dublin. I chose not to drive because I presumed I was getting a custodial sentence and wouldn't be driving home. We didn't say much on the trip up. The Criminal Courts of Justice building is a three-minute walk from the train station. We went straight to Court 16, where I met my solicitor and barrister. The case was called, and I sat in the dock. Justice Tony Hunt was the presiding judge. He greeted everyone in the room, me included, and proceeded to deliver his verdict. He read out the aggravating factors, the nature of the crime and my previous convictions. He then read the reports from the Probation Service and the treatment centre. Both were positive. He mentioned that I had repaid all €10,500 to the injured party and that I was still gainfully employed. He then spoke of the insidious nature of gambling addiction, and how it was becoming a danger to society in general. How right he was. Looking directly at me, he warned me in no uncertain terms that the chance he was about to give me was going to be my last. He sentenced me to four years' imprisonment. My heart sank. Then he said the magic words: suspended in full for ten years.

I nearly fell off my seat. I looked over at Dad, and I could see the blood returning to his face. I thanked the judge, my barrister and my solicitor, and I left the court.

As we were walking out the door, a pair of press photographers started taking photos of me. That meant that the media were taking a keen interest in the story, and I could expect the worst. This sent my dad into a rage. Then, on the steps of the court behind me, I caught a glimpse of the prosecuting garda. She didn't see me, but I remember her saying to someone on a phone call that 'the fat bastard walked. A fully suspended sentence.' We walked down to Parkgate Street and went into the first pub we could find. Dad called a pint for himself, and then he let me have it with both barrels.

He was worried about the publicity. More shame on him and the family. I couldn't blame him. But given the heat of the moment and the built-up tension, I argued with him. I stormed off and headed for the train station. When I got there, I was met with bad thing number two.

I was wandering around the concourse, waiting for the noon train. I presumed Dad would follow me over, and that we would both cool down on the trip home. I started to feel better. Then, a hand rested on my shoulder, and when I turned around it wasn't

Dad, but another garda. He told me that he was arresting me in connection with the false obtaining of betting vouchers from Paddy Power. If they couldn't get me one way, they were determined to get me another.

As I was getting into the patrol car, I could see my dad walking over the bridge approaching the station. I rolled down the window and told him that it was nothing to worry about and that I'd be home later.

The blood drained from his face again, and he just stood there, completely helpless and clueless.

My day had gone from me being a nervous wreck to being extremely relieved, from being elated and feeling euphoric to feeling like a piece of shit. And it wasn't yet midday.

We drove to the station in Blackrock. My solicitor had told me on many previous occasions to keep my mouth shut when being interviewed. This was something I never heeded, but on that day I felt a little bullish. And I had a sense of righteous indignation about this arrest. So I decided to not play ball for a change.

I started out well, answering every question asked of me with a firm 'no comment'. This lasted for a few hours. I had presumed that at the end of my six hours in custody, I would be released. I hadn't said anything and therefore hadn't incriminated myself, so I felt pretty good. Then they told me that they had just applied to their superintendent for a six-hour extension, with the option of keeping me 24 hours if they deemed it necessary. That was a game-changer. I was tired and quite emotional over the court case that morning, and all I wanted to do was get home, watch TV and catch up with my folks. Another contributing factor was that when the garda told me earlier that he had all his ducks in a row regarding this, he wasn't lying. He had a watertight case.

He told me that, if I played ball and gave a truthful statement, he'd release me and recommend to the Director of Public Prosecutions (DPP) that the matter be dealt with summarily in the District Court, which meant I could expect a lot more leniency than in the Circuit Court. I weighed up my options and decided to get it over and done with. I told him everything. I had committed this crime while on bail for the Bank of Ireland scam. I was totally out of control at this time. I had come up with what I had thought was a foolproof crime. I thought I could tell Paddy Power's marketing department that I needed to buy a large amount of betting vouchers for which they could invoice me through the company. They didn't question this, and over the course of a few weeks I obtained over €5,800 in vouchers, which, of course, I used to gamble the minute I got them. There were some winnings, but not much. After a month or so, when their accounts department noticed that the vouchers went unpaid, they reported me to the gardaí. He accepted that I was as cooperative as I could have been, and he was a man of his word. I was on the seven o'clock train home.

When I got home, I told Dad that it was an old matter they needed to clear up and that it was nothing to be worried about. Another lie. But I knew it would be a while before this matter went to court, and now that I was on the straight and narrow, I might get away with it too.

The next morning was great fun. I was headline news on the local radio. I had also made the *Daily Star*, *The Independent*, the *Daily Mail* and the local rag. It was all pictures, no sound at home for the remainder of the day. I felt really bad and embarrassed – not so much for myself, but for my family. I had disgraced them ... again. I should, of course, have felt bad for myself and worried about the damage I had done to myself, but I wasn't. I still had an element of self-loathing floating around somewhere in my psyche. But my overall feeling was one of happiness. I had survived the biggest court case I had ever faced and came out the other side relatively unscathed.

I went to work on the Wednesday morning. I was glad to get up to Dublin for a change. The few days away would allow the boiling pot to simmer, and when I got home at the weekend, the atmosphere would be better. I was also delighted to get to a GA meeting. I treasured my meetings. They were invaluable to me at this time, and I was really lucky to have found a few select meetings where all of the attending members were great guys. Trust is a massive thing at a recovery meeting: people share things that are very personal and sometimes dangerous to share. You have no control over what gets said back to people outside of the rooms. I have been to meetings over the years that undercover gardaí have attended under the guise of being recovering addicts, just to dig up information by listening to people sharing. That's about as immoral and unethical as it gets in my eyes.

I got home again on the evening of the following Friday. I went straight to a GA meeting and got home for ten o'clock. I was a little apprehensive because Friday nights were normally Dad's night for a few pints. Pints that didn't always agree with him and made him a little argumentative. Thankfully, he wasn't yet home, so after a chat with Mam, I went to bed and didn't even hear him come in. The next day, he was fine. We went to a match, and I drove him out to his homestead in County Clare that evening. He always really enjoyed that. And let's face it, it was the least I could do considering all the crap I had put him and my family through.

CHAPTER 22

A level of normalcy started to creep into my life after my court case ended. I found a healthy work–life balance with the three-day working week, and I had plenty of time to get stuck into my recovery. I had got close to a guy I was in treatment with – let's call him Alan – and we went to a lot of meetings and coffee mornings together. Of course, I still had the new court case hanging over me, and I wasn't sure when it would come up.

That issue was resolved in March 2011, and more strife was on its way. My resolve was certainly being tested, that's for sure. I was charged with obtaining betting vouchers fraudulently from Paddy Power plc. Thankfully the prosecuting garda was as good as his word, and the matter was dealt with at District Court level. I went to court confident for several reasons. Firstly, the maximum sentence I could get in the District Court was 18 months on a guilty plea; I could also appeal any sentence given and be released pending an appeal. Secondly, I felt that surely the judge was going to look at my case sympathetically, considering I was not long out of treatment and doing well. Thirdly, a higher court (Circuit) had recently decided not to jail me on a far more serious charge. I was also employed. I had a lot going in my favour.

The facts of the case were heard. The first problem was when the judge questioned whether I was liable for any winnings I may have accrued from fraudulently obtaining the vouchers. If so, I would have ended up with a figure of over ten grand as opposed to the €5,800 value of the vouchers. Thankfully, my solicitor argued against this and won the point. *One–nil to me*, I thought. Then came the real kick in the teeth.

The judge proceeded to tear strips off me. He closely examined my previous record and looked upon it with huge disdain. He made some very disparaging remarks about my character and stated that he wasn't going to fall for my defence of a gambling addiction, hinting that he was sick of people using addiction as an excuse to commit crimes. He sentenced me to 18 months' imprisonment – the maximum he could have given me. I was shell-shocked. He set bail at €1,000, which I didn't have, so I was taken to Cloverhill Prison. I instructed my solicitor to contact my family and tell them what had happened. Just when I thought I was getting my life back on track, the sins of my past had caught up with me. I felt like I was taking one step forward and three steps back.

At seven o'clock that evening, my sister arrived at the prison and posted my bail. I could tell that she wasn't happy, and I didn't know what to say to make the situation better. She drove me back to the court complex, where I collected my car. I thanked her, and she drove back home to Limerick. I felt like shit for making her feel the way she, and my other family members and close friends, did. I jumped in my car and drove straight to a GA meeting.

Life started to get better after that episode. I knew it would take at least a year for my appeal to be heard, given the backlog in the courts system. I was regularly attending my aftercare, going to GA meetings and meeting long-time members of other fellowships (like AA and NA) that I had gotten to know at Bushy Park. I had no inclination to gamble, and I was doing all of the recommended things – such as not reading the racing pages in the papers, not watching racing on TV and staying out of the pub on Saturday afternoons when there would be live racing on and lots of guys gambling. And it was working. I was starting to live again and was reasonably happy. I wasn't scared any more like I had been every time I saw a police car. And the reason for this was that I hadn't committed any crimes. It sounds easy, and it certainly made for a simple, hassle-free life, but to me, it was an alien feeling. I grew to like it, though, and the more I got involved with the right kind of people, the easier it became.

I was enjoying life at this time. There was no apprehension. I wasn't avoiding anybody, and I was something I wasn't very familiar with. I was happy. Between aftercare, GA meetings, work and socialising, my life was full. There weren't many free minutes in the day. I went out to Bushy Park every Sunday morning to meet the guys at the meeting and have coffee afterwards. As I write this, I realise how mundane it all sounds compared to a lot of the other content in this memoir. How I wish my life could have always been this mundane. I didn't have a care in the world, I wasn't getting into any trouble, and I was beginning to claw back some respect from those I had lost it with.

Time flew. Before I knew it, the year had passed. I got a phone call from my solicitor in Dublin: my appeal date had arrived. May 2012 in Court 16 in the Criminal Courts of Justice building. I felt confident, but you never quite know what way the cards will fall in these circumstances. I gathered as many references and reports as I could. I had glowing references from work and Bushy Park. I was also engaging well with the Probation Service. The judge took all of these reports into consideration and decided that she would adjourn the matter for 12 months. This was for two reasons. Firstly, she wanted to see if I could continue to stay out of trouble and make progress in rebuilding my life; and secondly, I still had to repay a large chunk of the compensation owed to Paddy Power.

I was happy enough with this outcome. It wasn't ideal, because I would have preferred if it had been finalised, instead of hanging over me for the next 12 months. But I guess that was the whole point of the adjournment: to keep me alert and aware of the potential consequences of any bad behaviour on my part. All in all, though, I was going home that afternoon, and that hadn't been a done deal that morning.

CHAPTER 23

've experienced many different emotions as a result of my addiction – elation, shame, depression and euphoria being the most prevalent. I never fully understood the mental ramifications my disease had on me. The idea that I could be mentally ill never occurred to me. The very thought of it horrified me. When I look back at the situations and danger I put myself in, being mentally unstable is probably the only logical explanation for a lot of the things I have done.

One particular incident brought it all home for me. Bizarrely, it involved nobody but me, and it terrified me at the time. It was a Saturday morning back when I was in the throes of my addiction, and I was at home in Limerick. I was under huge pressure to get cash. I don't recall if it was money I owed somebody or if I needed to pay for a trip, but I do remember feeling under more pressure than I normally was. It was fazing me, and that in itself should have been a warning that something was seriously wrong.

I drove into town in the late morning, parked the car and went on my merry way to the bookies. I remember that I needed somewhere in the region of €400 and had only €70 in my pocket. When I entered the bookies, I immediately started betting on whatever races were available to me. These included the morning greyhounds; South African, Indian and Australian racing; virtual racing (a particularly nasty and extremely addictive betting concept where you gamble on animated races); and some football that had early kick-offs. I spent a frenetic hour or so in there, winning some bets and losing others. It was incredibly frustrating. Normally, my betting streaks were either very bad or very good but seldom varied like this. The most I had in my pocket at any one time was €200 and the lowest was €30 – neither of which was going to solve my problem.

I decided that I was going to take the bull by the horns. I had €120 in my wallet. I looked at the next greyhound race and decided that the first dog I saw that was priced 3/1 was the one I would put the full €120 on. When it won, I would have €480, which was going to solve the problem. Easy. The race went off, and my dog fell out of the boxes. My bet was blown within five seconds.

I left the bookies in a complete tizzy. My head was spinning, and I was totally out of control. I decided that I was going to go home and mope for the rest of the weekend. My next problem came when I went to get my car – it wasn't there anymore. Just my luck, my bloody car was stolen. I went into a row of shops on the street where I had parked and asked each shop owner if they had seen any strange activity outside or heard a car being stolen. After all, it was midday on a Saturday, in the third-biggest city in Ireland, and I had parked in the city centre. People don't just steal cars in city centres in broad daylight in a busy shopping area, do they? Then again, this was me we're talking about. Anything could happen to me, and it wouldn't be unexpected.

I wandered around the surrounding streets looking for the car. It contained a lot of important work-related stuff like my laptop and some files, as well as a very expensive jacket. I just couldn't believe it. I realised that I had no choice but to call the gardaí and report it stolen. I was pretty sure that they would either find the theft rather amusing and ironic or think that it was part of an elaborate insurance scam on my behalf. By chance, I bumped into an off-duty garda that I knew quite well and told him what had happened. He told me to call it in, and then go straight up to the station to file an official report.

The call didn't take long, as the answering officer told me that he couldn't take details over the phone and that I'd need to show up in person. Reluctantly, I started to walk towards the station, really beating myself up and feeling sick on the double: not only had I not won the cash I needed, but I had also lost the one thing I relied upon most, my car. As I approached the station, I could see the post office in the distance. As I got to the post office, I looked across the road, and what was there to greet me but my car! Unharmed and parked safely. Then the flashbacks started.

I remembered it all now. Less than 90 minutes previously, I had driven to town and parked in this very spot. I had done so in order to run into the post office and do the lottery before I went gambling. But my head was so preoccupied with needing to win in the bookies, I had blanked everything else from my mind. The tizzy I had worked myself into in the bookies had caused me to forget where, a mere hour and a half earlier, I had parked my car.

I opened the door and sat behind the wheel. Before I could turn the key in the ignition, I found myself shaking – mildly at first, then uncontrollably. Tears started running from my eyes, and I cried like I had never cried before. I was scared – petrified, actually: I never felt so alone in my entire life. I genuinely thought I was losing the plot and going crazy. I don't know how long had passed, but some passers-by became concerned, and the next thing I knew, there were two gardaí knocking on my window, enquiring about my welfare. They were genuinely concerned and visibly upset by the story I told them. They wanted to know if they could call someone for me. When

I said no, one of them said that he would drive me home and get a patrol car to collect him to bring him back. That's how concerned he was. It was a nice thing to do, even though I was mortified by it at the time.

That's another example of what gambling did to me.

CHAPTER 24

By mid-2012, life was pretty good. It was largely non-eventful but good. I had a routine that I adhered to religiously, and it worked. I had designated meetings that I would attend like clockwork, my two-year aftercare was approaching its conclusion, I was still working a three-day week, and I was mixing with the kind of people that a recovering addict needs to be mixing with – other people in recovery who have long periods of abstinence behind them. I had a sponsor with whom I could talk about anything, and I had ever-improving relationships with my family and close friends.

One Sunday, my parents and my younger sister were having dinner. My dad didn't look too good. He had not been going to the pub as regularly as he usually did, and he didn't seem to have the same levels of interest in the things he loved doing. Something was wrong. My sister, who is a nurse, was quite concerned by his condition. She made some phone calls, and it was decided that Dad would need to go to hospital. As he had pretty good health insurance, we took him directly to a private hospital, the Galway Clinic.

My sister drove Dad to Galway, a relatively short one-hour drive. I stayed home with Mam, and we waited to hear from my sister. A few hours passed before she called, and when she did, she didn't have anything to report. They were keeping him in for further tests and wouldn't make any determinations until then. My sister had been speaking to the consultant, however, and he wasn't optimistic about what they might find. The next morning would tell a tale.

I drove Mam to Galway the next morning, and we all waited for the test results. The omens were not good. On my dad's side of the family, there was a history of cancer. His brother died from pancreatic cancer at just 48 years of age. His dad, my grandfather Paddy, died at the same age before I was born; another of his brothers died at 50, and a sister at 61. Dad was 67, a relatively young man, and he had been in relatively good shape up to this point.

Later that morning, the consultant spoke to us: the scans and colonoscopy showed a tumour in Dad's bile duct, a relatively rare place to occur. He left us to discuss the options. The first issue we had was that we had doubts about leaving him in Galway. None of us had gotten a good vibe from the consultant we spoke to, and it was decided that all further treatment would be done elsewhere. After some research, it was decided that St Vincent's Private Hospital in Dublin would be the place to go. A consultation was set up with Mr Emir Hoti, who had an outstanding reputation in pancreatic and liver surgery. This was going to cost an arm and a leg, so it was a godsend that my parents always had paid a generous annual premium to the Vhi. It was certainly going to come in handy over the next 16 months.

I have to admit that I found the whole situation with Dad very upsetting. My mother seemed to be handling it just fine, but she was a past master at not showing emotion and hiding her feelings. What I did notice was that she developed a different attitude towards Dad. Their relationship, which had been on the go for well over 50 years at this stage, was pretty much as you'd expect from any relationship that had survived that long. They both got on with things. But now, I noticed that whenever Dad wasn't around, Mam was talking about him a lot more and reminiscing. To me, this was a sign that she was struggling as much as I was with the situation, but I also knew that it wasn't something she was ever going to talk about with anyone. All I could do was be there when and if she needed me.

The opportunity of a job at home also appeared at this time. A long-term client had a tyre distributor in Limerick that was struggling, and they asked if I'd go in and lend some of my experience to try and refloat the ship. The money wasn't very good at all, but the pros outweighed the cons. I'd be permanently back at home, where I was needed, and it was a new challenge. I didn't take much convincing.

Around this time, I was just finishing my two-year aftercare programme. It went well, and I gained a lot from it. When in the treatment centre for a meeting one Sunday morning, my counsellor Pat asked me in for a cup of tea and a chat. I spoke to her about Dad, and what my fears were. I told her about the new job, which she was pleased about, as she was always trying to get me home out of Dublin. I could always chat to Pat, and I hung on her every word. She was, at this time, one of the most important people in my life, and I valued her opinions and insights greatly. I'd go as far as to say that if she had told me to jump through hoops, I would have hopped to it straight away. At the end of the conversation, she asked me if I'd consider giving something back to the centre. I wasn't sure how I could do this, as I wasn't in a good place financially. But it wasn't financial help she was after. She wanted me to do a training course to facilitate future aftercare groups.

I was a bit taken aback by this – I believed that I didn't have the experience. Pat pointed out to me that the best facilitators are recovering addicts, and that someone with my experiences of gambling would be invaluable to future groups. It didn't take me long to make up my mind – if Pat thought I was capable of doing it, then

I was capable of doing it. I told her to put my name down and to send me the details. It got me thinking of my aftercare group, and its facilitators Seamus and Liz. They were incredible, and the way they ran the group was fantastic.

The training for facilitators started in October 2012. It ran over the course of six weekends, and lasted all of Saturday and Sunday, from 9 a.m. to 5 p.m. It was attended by 11 others, many of whom I already knew, either through meetings or treatment. It was intense training, and it was brilliantly taught by a lady named Ellen, who was the aftercare coordinator at Bushy Park.

Facilitators are people who have an understanding of the illness of addiction through their own experience of being an addict or having a family member who is one. The underlying approach is one of treating people with understanding, dignity and positive regard, so a non-judgemental attitude is essential.

The role of the facilitator is to ensure the guidelines for the Continuum of Care programme are adhered to, thus providing a safe and consistent space for all involved. The core function of the facilitator is to listen, support, observe and ensure the groups are run in accordance with the standards required.

The training is done in collaboration with the Irish College of Humanities and Applied Science (ICHAS), and its goal is to provide the necessary training in group skills and facilitation with an award of QQI Level 6. Being a facilitator is an amazing experience. It's not always the easiest thing to do, but it's hugely rewarding watching someone rebuild their life and grow into a person unshackled from addiction.

It was a privilege to be part of a fellow addict's journey of recovery, to experience their concerns first-hand and to see how they coped, changed and grew while embracing the 12-Step programme. It was hugely rewarding to me and gave me gratitude for where I was and for the help that I received in my aftercare group with Seamus and Liz and the others in recovery.

I really enjoyed those six weekends. They provided me with a great distraction from the pain and turmoil I was feeling due to Dad being sick, and they helped me greatly in my recovery. They also led to a whole new circle of friends, some of whom I am still in contact with today.

The job with the tyre distributor was more enjoyable than I had thought, and I enjoyed waking up in my own bed every morning and coming home every evening. The pay wasn't great – it was substantially less than what I was earning in Dublin – but when you factor in the cost of living in Dublin compared to Limerick, it wasn't that bad. Also, I was doing pretty well with my recovery – I hadn't had a bet in almost two and a half years; as a result, money wasn't my God. I could comfortably live on my new wage. It was a strange feeling, but a very good one.

Christmas was going to be strange. Normally it would have entailed two major elements for me: gambling and socialising. This year, there wouldn't be any gambling, which was great; however, sadly, I wouldn't be able to share a pint with Dad on Christmas morning, either. He had just had the first of a few major surgeries to remove the tumour in his bile duct, and he was undergoing serious chemotherapy. It meant that going to the pub was a big no-no for him. I think that this affected him greatly. He loved his pints, but he lived for the social interaction in the pub, too. The banter over the GAA and Man United, and the local rivalry between our rugby club,

Shannon, and Young Munster were always huge focal points in the pub and provided great entertainment.

I felt so sorry for him. It broke my heart to see him like this, and I know that he was both scared and humiliated by the whole thing, too. He was a very proud man, always well-groomed and pristine. I had never seen him with more than one day of stubble prior to this. Now he was looking sickly, losing weight and developing a sallow, gaunt appearance. But no matter how he looked or felt, one thing I knew for sure was that he was going to fight the cancer and fight it with every fibre in his body. As I mentioned earlier, Dad had an incredible work ethic, and he brought that into this disease. He was going to beat it, no matter what it took. That was his attitude, and I couldn't help but develop a new sense of admiration for him because of it.

I spoke earlier about the concept of a higher power and its importance in recovery. Dad had his own higher power in this battle, even though he probably didn't realise it. It came in the form of my niece Katie, who has been close to death herself a few times as a result of being born prematurely. Dad IDOLISED Katie – that's the only word I can use, and I can't capitalise it enough. She was a huge part of his life. Over the long periods he spent in hospital, whenever I visited him, the first question he asked was always, 'How's my little Katie?'

Like anyone with a terminal diagnosis, Dad's life became a roller-coaster. He had really good days when you wouldn't even know he was sick; there were what I used to call the so-so days when he would experience highs and lows; and then there were the really bad days when he couldn't even get out of bed because of sheer weakness, pain and exhaustion. But the dogged determination that he was going to beat it was a constant. That never wavered, and I loved him for it.

The new job asked me to go to Stoke, in England, for a couple of weeks. They had a subsidiary company over there that wasn't performing well. By the time I finished my appraisal, I knew that 'not performing well' was a massive understatement. It was haemorrhaging money at a rate of knots. The Stoke company had to be shut down, and any assets it had needed to be liquidated quickly. This meant that I was going to have to spend at least another four weeks there. I would travel over on Sunday nights and return home on Friday nights. There was a direct flight from Shannon to Manchester, and I'd have a rental car waiting for me. I enjoyed the challenge of the work. It was intense and time-consuming. I'd work from 6 a.m. to 6 p.m. every day, and I was able to find a GA meeting on Tuesday, Wednesday and Thursday nights.

In total, I spent almost six weeks in Stoke. But every day I spent there – in fact, every hour I spent there – my mind was elsewhere. It was mostly thinking about Dad, how he was and how Mam was coping with it all. But there was also someone else on my mind. Towards the winter of that year, I had met a woman who would turn my whole world upside down.

Fiona.

CHAPTER 25

When I was in treatment a couple of years previously, I had gotten quite friendly with another resident, Ruth, and we had remained good friends on the outside, often speaking on the phone and going to the same meetings. After these meetings, we'd regularly go for coffee and a chat. Early on in her recovery, Ruth had been a mess. I'm delighted to say that today she is the exact opposite and is doing very well.

Every recovering addict is encouraged to find a sponsor as soon as they possibly can. A sponsor in any support organisation like AA or GA is someone who can help guide you through the recovery programme and, specifically, the 12 Steps. This person is generally someone who has a good amount of sobriety or abstinence under their belt, and who feels comfortable guiding others through difficult times in their recovery. A sponsor is an understanding and sympathetic person whom you can trust and turn to with problems associated not only with recovery but with life in general. Sponsorship is a vital tool for the 12-Step pathway of recovery. Although there are no formal sponsorship rules, it's recommended that a sponsor has at least one to two years of sobriety before they begin to sponsor.

One day in the autumn of 2012, after a meeting, Ruth was visibly upset. I suggested that she should speak to her sponsor immediately. She called her there and then, and conveniently, her sponsor was in a coffee shop literally two minutes away from where we were. I advised Ruth to go and talk to her, said goodbye and went towards my car.

She called after me and asked me to go with her, as she was still quite upset. I reluctantly agreed.

When we got to the coffee house, there were a lot of people sitting outside, as it was a nice day. I was a bit apprehensive since this was a mostly female environment, and I thought that they might be best left to themselves. Two ladies were sitting on high stools, engrossed in conversation, a cigarette and a cup of coffee. Ruth approached these ladies and embraced the one who was sitting with her back to me. After a minute, Ruth composed herself and introduced us. The petite raven-haired lady spun around and introduced herself with the most dazzling smile I have ever seen. Instantly, I felt like I did when I had my first crush as a fourteen-year-old. My palms became clammy, and I struggled to introduce myself because I was tongue-tied. Right there and then, I knew that this lady was special. We spoke briefly, and then I made my excuses and left. My head was in a spin, I had butterflies in my stomach, and I was afraid that I was not only out of my depth but likely to make a complete ass of myself.

I drove home, and for the entire 40-minute journey – and the rest of that day – I couldn't get this lady named Fiona out of my head.

The next few weeks passed pretty uneventfully. Dad was home recuperating after the surgery, and he was putting as positive a spin on things as he possibly could. Work was rolling along, and it was quite enjoyable. I was facilitating my own aftercare group every Monday night. It was a very different, insightful experience. Being in the same chair as Seamus and Liz, my facilitators when I was in aftercare, was somewhat daunting. I felt like I had huge shoes to fill, but I was given every assurance by Ellen, the coordinator, Pat, my counsellor, and other friends in the fellowships that I'd be more than capable of filling them.

It was a nervous start. I was very anxious not to say the wrong thing at the wrong time. But that worked in my favour. The key to being a good group facilitator is being a good listener. It's not about the facilitator: it's about the member in early recovery. Some groups have been destroyed by overzealous facilitators who are all too keen to impress their own opinions and experiences on the group. This can have a detrimental effect – not only on an individual but on the group dynamic as a whole. Seamus and Liz are two of the most zen, energy-filled people I have ever met. In two years, they never once raised their voices in any session, allowing the meetings to flow effortlessly. This wasn't an easy thing to do. Our group often got very volatile, bordering on aggressive, yet they handled every situation perfectly. This was how I tried to work with my group. My co-facilitator was a little too fond of the sound of his own voice for my liking, and at times we probably came across as a 'good cop, bad cop' partnership, but it seemed to work, so that was good.

Every fellowship has an annual convention in its own county, and people from other areas will travel to conventions countrywide. These conventions are nice occasions, with large crowds and marathon sessions of meetings and workshops all through the weekend. Since I had been in treatment in County Clare, and since a lot of my meetings were also there, I attended an AA convention in Ennis with some friends who were recovering alcoholics. There was a dance on the Saturday night. When I got there, around seven o'clock, the hotel was packed with recovering addicts. There was a lot of chatting going on. Around an hour in, I went for a wander around the hotel to see who was there. Then, from the corner of my eye, I saw a hand waving at me. I didn't know who it was, because my distance vision wasn't great (even with glasses), but when I approached, I was delighted to see that it was Fiona who was beckoning me. She was there with a friend, drinking coffee.

When I had first seen Fiona, a few weeks previously, she had swept me off my feet. Now she looked even better, if that was at all possible. The way she smiled at me, the way she looked at me ... everything about her just melted me there and then. She invited me to join them for a coffee, and the next three hours simply flew by. We chatted about a whole host of different things, and I loved every minute of it.

At the end of the evening, I didn't have the guts to ask Fiona for her phone number. I still thought that she was way out of my league and that I hadn't a snowball's chance in hell that she'd ever be interested in me.

A few weeks passed after the convention. Life was going on in a mostly routine fashion. Dad was getting chemotherapy, and he seemed to be taking to it reasonably well. He was still very sick, though. It was as clear as the nose on your face that he wasn't right, and we were having to look at the possibility that he wasn't going to beat this thing.

Work was plodding along. I was glad I had decided to take the job closer to home. The fact that I wasn't gambling made it easier to live on the reduced salary. Socially, things were good, and I felt that I had created a very good social balance between my lifelong friends and the friends I had made in recovery.

Ruth called me one afternoon, in a pretty distressed state. We had a good chat, but I was genuinely worried about her. She was very close to taking a drink, and that, for someone like Ruth, may well have been fatal. Because some of her issues were of a female nature, I was a little lost as to how I could help her. I suggested that she speak to Fiona, as Fiona was her sponsor, a woman and far better equipped to help. Ruth said that she was too embarrassed to speak to Fiona and wanted to know if I'd speak to her first, to broker a meeting between them. I explained that I didn't know Fiona very well and had no way of contacting her. Ruth asked if she could give Fiona my number and have her call me. I agreed, and not only was Ruth happy with this, but I was secretly delighted that Fiona would be calling me. This would give me a way in with her. I felt bad in a way. This felt like an underhand way of getting in touch with her, but to hell with that! Feeling bad didn't last long.

The call came a couple of days later, on a Saturday evening. I can even remember where I was when it came through: waiting for a pizza at Domino's in Ennis. I asked if I could call her back in a few minutes and did so when I was back in the car. I explained the situation with Ruth to her, and she said that she'd take care of that. We then continued to chat for a while: small talk about how we both were and how I was enjoying being a facilitator. (Fiona had been one herself for many years.) Towards the end of the conversation, I heard something that I really didn't want to hear. Fiona told me that she was currently in a relationship. I knew that she had been married, and I wondered for a bit if this was what she was referring to, but it soon became clear that this was not the case. If you can imagine a hot-air balloon soaring through the clouds that suddenly deflates and comes crashing down to earth with a bang, then you can understand how I felt. Deep down, I had always known that this was a probability, albeit one that I didn't want to acknowledge. There was, however, a little chink of light at the end of the tunnel: Fiona told me that the relationship wasn't working, and without her going into too much detail, I got the impression that she wasn't happy.

I was in with a shot there, and I was going to make sure that she knew I'd be there for her. We agreed to stay in touch.

Christmas 2012 was upon us. While I was very happy with most facets of my life, especially the romantic pursuit of Fiona, the situation with Dad was deteriorating. We were called to a family consultation with Mr Hoti in mid-December, and the news we were given wasn't at all good. The prognosis was that Dad had between nine and twelve months to live, barring miracles. We all handled the news in different ways. Mam was her usual stoic self. She didn't show much in the way of emotion, but I knew that, inside, she was devastated. My sisters are very different people in a lot of ways. The older one takes very much after her paternal grandmother. There's a steeliness about her, and she can be very clinical. She seemed to deal with all of this in a way befitting those attributes. My younger sister is the polar opposite. She's very hands-on and quite emotional. She also works in healthcare, and she was able to explain the ins and outs of medical jargon. I think I am somewhere in between, as you might expect from the middle child. I might come across as confident and assertive, but inside I was an emotional wreck. The whole situation was truly horrific, for all of us.

From a gambling perspective, life couldn't be better. I hadn't had a bet for almost two and a half years, and any thoughts or urges to do so seemed well and truly suppressed. This was largely down to adhering to my recommended recovery plan. Every morning, I repeated the 'People, Places and Things' mantra to myself. If you associate with the right kind of people (those in recovery or those who have a strongly positive effect on your daily life), stay away from the wrong kind of places (places that might tempt you into relapse, like in my case a betting shop) and avoid things that can help you to have a bet (like carrying cash or buying newspapers with racing pages), then life tends to flow a lot easier. This was proving to be the case with me.

I was very lucky to have been taken under the wing of a man named John, whom I had met at the Sunday morning meetings while I was in treatment. John had a pretty tragic backstory. Alcohol had ravaged him and taken everything he had – and I mean everything. It cost him his marriage, his relationship with his kids was seriously damaged, he'd lost his farm (which was worth a small fortune) and physically he wasn't in good shape as a result of his drinking. John hadn't taken a drink in over 20 years, one day at a time. His attitude, and gratitude, inspired me every time I met him. We would get together a few times a week for coffee and speak on the phone on the days we wouldn't meet.

The main thing I admired about John was that he never let me rest on my laurels. He constantly reminded me of the reality of being an addict, and that it didn't matter how long you were clean, sober or bet-free. Every new dawn brought the potential for our disease to awaken inside us and devour us whole. John saw things in me that I thought I was doing a great job of hiding. He saw my arrogance. He saw my complacency. He saw my vulnerability. And he wasn't backwards in coming forward when he felt I needed to be brought down a peg or two. But conversely, he would congratulate me every day on not having a bet. He would also praise the positive things I was doing in my recovery.

Sadly, I'm not in contact with John today, largely through faults of my own. I still think of him every day and will always be grateful to him.

*

The friend in my adversity I shall always cherish most. I can better trust those who helped to relieve the gloom of my dark hours than those who are so ready to enjoy with me the sunshine of my prosperity.

Ulysses S. Grant

One thing that I have been truly blessed with in my life is the relationship I have with my friends. An old adage comes to mind: 'You can see who your true friends are when the chips are down.' Well, we have all been close for over 30 years, and during that time the chips have well and truly been down. Yet, I have never truly appreciated my friends until recently. I've had hundreds of acquaintances, but only five real friends. It's taken me a long time to realise this. They know who they are, and I don't have to name them. What I will say is that there's a distinct probability that I would not be alive today were it not for them.

Each of us is very different in many ways, but oh so similar in others. One is a rock of sense, pragmatic and somewhat overly sensible. He wasn't always like this but has become so. Then we have one who's a little bit of everything – both sensible and pragmatic; he has a dry wit and can be hilariously funny and sloppy at the same time. Then there's the 'young fella' ... a lad that everyone likes even though he's as subtle as a brick and as blunt as a rusty butter knife. There's the old fella, or 'Da' as we all know him. We've been on many road trips and life adventures over the years. He has an acerbic sense of humour and can be a tad grumpy. But, as the 'young fella' says, 'Da's a grump, but he's our grump!'

Then there's 'Al Bundy', as in Al Bundy from the hilarious 1990s TV show *Married with Children*. A man who breezes through life as if he hasn't a care in the world. I've yet to meet a person who has had a bad word to say about our 'Al Bundy'. That says it all about him, really.

I'm ashamed to say that I have treated these five friends appallingly at times over the past 30 years. I've promised them things I couldn't get. I've borrowed money from them. I've put them all in positions where they found themselves defending me to people when I was completely indefensible. Yet they all have stood by me, right up to the present day. There must be something wrong with all of them. Or perhaps there isn't. For a long time, it never occurred to me that these guys are, quite simply, a bunch of really great people.

We have travelled together to matches and holidays. We have laughed together and cried together. I've been through my best days with these guys, and through my darkest. I have no right to expect the levels of friendship and loyalty they constantly show me. But they're always there, and I am eternally grateful for them.

Thank you.

CHAPTER 26

January 2013 came around – the beginning of yet another year. For me, it would be a very tumultuous year and one that I will never forget, for reasons both good and bad. Actually, forget about 'good and bad' – you can replace those words with 'incredible and tragic'. The incredible part involved my love life and Fiona. The tragic part involved the passing of my dad.

The year started well. Dad was showing positive signs of potential recovery. I was working hard and enjoying it. I was over and back from the UK on a project, still working as a facilitator, and a million miles removed from having a bet. I had been talking more and more with Fiona on the phone. Mostly, either of us would use a recovery-related issue as an excuse to make the call. Once this 'issue' was discussed, we would talk about life in general.

It was during one of these calls that she confirmed that she was still in a relationship. She told me this around late January. To say I was gutted was an understatement; however, I wasn't that surprised. I had always thought that I was attempting the impossible in thinking I had a shot with her. I tried to shrug it off and not let it bother me. But it did. It really did.

The following week I got a call from Fiona, who was travelling from a funeral in Dundalk with some colleagues of hers. She asked me if I fancied meeting them for a coffee in Durty Nelly's, a popular pub in Bunratty, midway between Ennis and Limerick. For some reason, I declined. I can't remember why, but I'm sure that if she had asked me to meet her alone, I'd have jumped at the chance. I made some excuse and left it at that.

I was intrigued the next day, and in a bit of a quandary. Since Fiona had told me that she was in a relationship, I had decided to try and distance myself from the situation. I had fallen hard for this woman – harder than I'd ever fallen for anyone in the past. I knew that I wouldn't be able to do the 'let's be friends' thing. It would have been too hard. Then, that evening, after a GA meeting in Ennis, her name appeared on my mobile phone caller display. Christ, she wasn't making this easy. I answered. She asked how I was and if I was in Ennis, as she knew I regularly went to meetings in Bushy Park or The Friary. I told her that I was, and I was just about to head home. She then surprised me by asking me to call up to her house. She said that she could really do with a chat. I tried to disguise the delight in my voice when I told her I would, and my heart was pounding as she gave me directions to her house. I had no idea what this was about and tried hard to keep things in perspective. But I couldn't shake *that* feeling – the one you get when you're a teenager who has his first crush. I stopped off at a local shop and got some coffees and cakes as I knew she had a fondness for both.

When I got there, Fiona was waiting for me at the door. She invited me in, but something was troubling about her demeanour. She thanked me for the coffee and cake, and we sat idly for a few minutes – me, making silly small talk, and she, sitting on the edge of her seat. I could see that she was bothered about something, so I just came out and asked her if everything was alright. Her reply shocked me.

The first thing she told me was that she was going to Texas to be with her sister for a few weeks. I interpreted this as there being something wrong with her sister, so I asked if she was okay. It transpired that the problem wasn't with her sister. Fiona needed to get away from her boyfriend. It turned out that the guy was nothing short of an uncaged animal with a propensity for violence against women, and Fiona had been the latest victim in a long line. She went through everything: how she had met him, started to date him, and how and when things had started to turn nasty. It was a truly horrific tale, one that involved coercive control, shocking violence and seemingly endless manipulation and intimidation. What I was looking at there in front of me wasn't the gorgeous, radiant woman I had met a few months earlier. It was a broken, beaten-down woman who was petrified. It appalled me. We just sat there for a few hours. I listened as Fiona poured her heart out, and I drove home later, bewildered.

At this time, my life had developed a very set pattern. If one was to analyse this pattern, one might say that it was regimented, bordering on boring. But it suited me. I was thriving in the company of others in recovery. The facilitation work was very rewarding, and most importantly, I was getting great benefit from my GA meetings. I had not had a bet in almost three years, one day at a time. In terms of gambling, nothing was hanging over me, no albatrosses.

What was hanging over me was Dad's illness. With every passing day, things were getting worse. There was a period in early February when he started to think that he was getting better. This misconception proved to be very bad for him. He went to town one morning on the bus, saying that he fancied a stroll now that he was feeling a bit better. When Mam rang me at 3 p.m. that afternoon, I sensed something was wrong. She rarely, if ever, called me; if she did, it was to bring her shopping, but I had done that the night before. It turned out that Dad had dropped into his local and felt good enough to chance a pint of his beloved Guinness.

Before he got sick, Dad had always found it difficult to drag himself away from the pub. He called it the Glue Pot. He loved the banter. Patsy's is the number-one sporting pub in Limerick: you couldn't sit at the bar in Patsy's and not find yourself engaged in a conversation about the GAA. Dad's beloved Clare were on a bit of a roll in 2013, and he loved being able to take the moral high ground now that the Banner were top dogs. One pint turned into three, and they were going down well. The next thing we knew was that he was curled up in bed, violently ill.

I felt so, so sorry for him. Not because of the effect the drink had on him, not because he had cancer, but because his life was being taken from him. Slowly and painfully, he was being deprived of all the things he lived for. He could no longer go out and socialise with his friends. He could no longer eat and enjoy his favourite foods. He wasn't able to go to the Six Nations games with us, or any other matches. And, most damaging of all to him, he couldn't spend the same amount of quality time with Katie, the grandchild that he idolised.

Mr Hoti had warned us at a family conference in December 2012 that, given the gravity of Dad's condition, recovery was unlikely, and he had estimated that he had around 12 months left. When he told us this, it didn't sink in. Looking at Dad now, how sick he was, it was starting to. His steely fight and determination were leaving him. When they finally went, I knew that he would go too.

The support I was getting around this time was phenomenal. My ever-present pillars, my lifelong friends, were always there for me – to listen to me pouring my heart out, to go for a pint or to talk shite about sport and women. But I also had the friends I had made in recovery. Their support was invaluable, as they were the ones who really understood addiction. Their caring about me was beautiful and overwhelming. It wasn't all pats on the back and hugs telling me everything was going to be alright. It was a lot of direct, logical and practical advice mixed with compassion. I needed this to keep my feet, and my head, firmly grounded. They knew that there was self-destruction around the corner at all times for any recovering addict, no matter what one's circumstances are. I had already self-destructed before after a very long period of strong recovery, so it would be very easy to do so again.

A fortnight had passed since Fiona went to Texas to stay with her sister. She was very much in my thoughts, but the pessimist in me was ever-present. I doubted if she would ever even return home, given the state in which she'd left the country. Then, to my surprise, one afternoon at work, I got a ping from my phone telling me that I had unopened emails. There, five or six down on the list, was one from Fiona. Immediately, the butterflies started fluttering in my stomach. I paused before opening it, full of excitement and trepidation at the same time. Was she writing to tell me that she was staying in Texas? Was she writing to tell me that she had met someone new over there and fallen for him?

I finally mustered up the courage to open the email. She told me that everything was fine. Her sister, also a recovering alcoholic, had brought her to meetings, and she had found a support group for women who suffered abuse at the hands of their partners. She was happy and getting the help she needed. I was delighted for her, and I could tell from her phraseology that she was in a much better place mentally than when she had boarded that plane two weeks ago.

But while I was delighted, I was also quite sad. What if she didn't want to come home? Had my usefulness to her now expired? The last paragraph answered my questions. She told me that she would never be able to repay me for what I did for her and that she was so very grateful for it all. She said that she was coming home in a week and was looking forward to catching up. She knew that it was my birthday soon and wanted to know if she could take me out to dinner to say thanks and celebrate.

I re-read the email at least ten times after that. I flagged it as 'important' so it would stay at the top of my inbox and always be the first one I saw when I logged on. Driving home from work that afternoon, I felt like a kid with a crazy crush that had just snagged a date with the cute girl. I was euphoric.

Fiona was due to touch down at Shannon Airport on the last Thursday in February. It was my birthday the following Saturday. While I was looking forward to seeing her, I figured that she wouldn't be in touch for a week or so, until she settled back in at home. Every time my phone rang on Thursday caused me to stop whatever I was doing and frantically look at the screen in the hope that it was her. I received many calls, but none from Fiona.

Friday brought about even further distraction: I couldn't concentrate at work due to a combination of worry about Dad and hope that she might call. On my way home that evening, the magic words I had been hoping for finally appeared on my screen: 'Fiona calling'. I got every bit as much of a euphoric high when I saw her name as I did after a really big win in the bookies. This threw me slightly. Suddenly, my head started to fill with doubts. *What are you doing? You're way out of your league here.* Thoughts along these lines were rampant. I let the phone ring out rather than answer it. I didn't know what to say or do.

I got home about 20 minutes later and received a text from Fiona saying that she had tried to call me, that she hoped I was well, and to call her when I could. I fought like crazy to stop myself from calling her straight back. I needed to be cool about this and not come across as a bungling idiot. I ate some dinner, showered and sat with Dad for an hour. Then I made the call.

When she answered, my heart melted. Even her voice gave me butterflies. We chatted for a long time. She told me that she felt much better and that the break was just what she needed. She had missed her parents and her daughter, but she seemed really happy. I didn't want to push the dinner invitation. After all, I wasn't sure if she still wanted to, having had three weeks to think about it. Then, just as we were about to bid each other goodnight, she asked me if I had any birthday plans. When I told her that my days of celebrating birthdays were well behind me, she laughed and asked me if I wanted to have dinner with her the next night. I jokingly told her that I'd have to check my diary, then immediately that I'd love to. We arranged a time and place, and as they say, the rest is history.

I went back in to say goodnight to Dad after that call. It seemed that every time I looked at him now, he was deteriorating further. I remember going to bed both the happiest and saddest I had been in a long time.

On 2 March 2013, I woke up with a spring in my step. I had reached the ripe old age of 44. At times, over the past few years, I had felt like I was a hundred on my birthday. I had allowed gambling to consume every fibre of my being for so long, it seemed to have left an indelible mark. But not today. I had a date that night, the best birthday present I could have asked for, with the possible exception of a cure for cancer. I got up, showered, had a nice breakfast and collected my little nephews. They loved going to the cinema, and whenever there was a film that they wanted to see, Uncle Buck (yours truly) got to take them. That moniker had come from my mother years ago, given my physical similarity to John Candy and his role in the movie of the same name. My nieces and nephews loved it and found it hilarious. I recall little Katie getting very confused one time when Dad called me Patrick when addressing me. She quickly admonished him, reminding Ganga (grandad) that my name was Buck, not Patrick!

I watched a rugby game in the pub in the afternoon, then I went home to get ready. I had arranged to meet Fiona in a very nice gastropub in Bunratty. I was nervous as hell, but it was an exciting nervousness. We pulled into the car park at the same time and greeted each other with a hug and a peck on the cheek. Fiona looked even better than she had when we had met previously. We spent the next three hours chatting about Texas, how she was feeling now, my dad, our jobs … pretty much everything and anything. The time just flew. At the end of the evening, I didn't know what to do next. Should I kiss her? If so, on the cheek or the lips? Should I ask for another date? I really didn't know. For a finish, we hugged and promised each other that we'd contact each other very soon. It felt strange. I was neither inflated nor deflated. But I was happy. As I was getting into my car, I saw her walking over towards mine. She had something in her hand. I rolled down the window, and she handed me a small box and a card, wished me a happy birthday and kissed me on the cheek. The big smile on her face told me that she was happy too.

I waited until she'd driven off to open the box. Inside was a little toy paperweight for my desk at work, and a card wishing me a fantastic birthday and thanking me for everything I had done for her. I drove home as happy as the cat that got the cream.

After my birthday date, things took off rather quickly. Fiona and I texted and spoke on the phone a few times, and she invited me up for a coffee on a Thursday night after my GA meeting in Ennis. After a lot of small talk, we finally got round to addressing the elephant in the room: I told her about my feelings, and she admitted that she had feelings for me too. But she was worried that it might be too soon for her, and she said that she was very wary of men since her ordeal at the hands of the ex. I told her that I understood, and that I would give her whatever space she needed.

I was in bed that night when my phone rang shortly after midnight. This both woke me and worried me. I wasn't in the habit of either making or receiving phone calls at this hour, and I thought there might be something wrong. In a sleepy haze, I fumbled around under the pillow for my phone, and saw Fiona's name appear on the screen. The first thing that flashed through my mind was that the violent ex had been bothering her again. When I answered the phone, I expected her to be in a flustered state at the other end of the line, but she was calm and apologetic. She was sorry for waking me, but she had something she needed to tell me, and it needed to be said straightaway.

My heart sank, as I awaited the gentle letdown. The 'it's not you, it's me' chat. However, to my amazement, Fiona told me that she felt the same way I did, and that if I was prepared to be tolerant of what she was going through, she wanted to take things further. I couldn't believe my ears. A funny thing then happened: my dad let a shout out to keep the noise down as he was trying to get some sleep. That brought out a little laugh from me. There was life in the grumpy old fecker yet.

CHAPTER 27

Life with Fiona was everything I thought it would be. It was intense. Initially, I was full of insecurity, constantly doubting myself and wondering what she was doing with a guy like me. After all, she was gorgeous and not short of admirers, from what I could gather from the way people spoke about her; I was broke, seriously overweight and not exactly an oil painting. But it worked.

The next few months would see us become inseparable. Within weeks of the relationship beginning, I was given a key to Fiona's house and I had practically moved in. I wasn't really aware of this until my mother remarked one afternoon that it was 'a pleasure to see me' and joked that she was surprised that I remembered where she lived. In hindsight, this was typical addict behaviour, probably from both of us. We were just so wrapped up in each other that we failed to see it. We were oblivious to all around us and happy living in our own little bubble. This was all I had wanted all of my life: a loving relationship with a beautiful woman, a decent job and my family not having to worry about me. It's easy for me to look back now and see where and why things went so wrong, but after living the type of life I had for so long, it was impossible not to grab on to this perception of bliss and hold on for dear life.

While my life with Fiona was delightful, life for Dad was getting worse all the time. By July 2013, he had moved more or less permanently to St Vincent's Hospital in Dublin. This, although an ominous move, was the best possible place for him, and I cannot speak highly enough of the levels of care and attention he received there. The staff – from the head of the department Professor Hoti right down the scale – were friendly, courteous and sympathetic, and they would do whatever they could for you.

I also got a lucky break on the job front at this time. I was headhunted by a large sales outsourcing consultancy and offered a position that gave me greater flexibility and a substantial pay rise. I explained the situation with Dad to them, and they were amazing. They agreed that I could defer my start date until October, but they'd put me on the books straightaway. This allowed me to spend a large amount of time with Dad. Fiona and I would go and stay in Dublin at the weekends, so I had a most welcome distraction from what was going on in St Vincent's.

Mam came to Dublin a couple of times a week to see Dad. She would never show any emotion, but I knew that this was devastating for her. They had argued more than Jack and Vera Duckworth in their day, but they were together for over 50 years. She hated hospitals, and you could almost feel the dread from her every time we drove through the car park. She knew that things were coming to an end. I guess deep down we all did.

By the end of September, the cancer was ravaging Dad, and Professor Hoti had to have 'the talk' with us. Mam, my sisters and I were summoned to a family conference on a Thursday morning. Professor Hoti couldn't dress what he had to tell us up in a fancy outfit and make it look good. He told us, in a most compassionate way, that Dad's time was up, and that he would pass on his own terms, in his own time. It was nothing we weren't expecting to hear, yet hearing it made me feel like I had been hit by a truck travelling at the speed of light. It took a while for it to sink in, for all of us, and when it did, we went up to see Dad and pretended it was just another day.

The next move was to arrange accommodation for him, and we all agreed that Dad would go to Milford Hospice. Milford is the most remarkable place. It was founded in 1928 by the Little Company of Mary Sisters, and it provides care for the elderly, as well as palliative care for those with a terminal illness. It goes over and above when it comes to caring for those in need, but what is remarkable is that it cares just as much about the families of those it nurses. Another remarkable thing is that Milford accepts everyone. It is not discriminatory, nor does it look at your bank balance or property portfolio before giving you a bed. It is funded through donations by amazing people like J.P. McManus and fundraisers of different types throughout the year.

However, there is a certain stigma attached to it. When someone is sick and ends up in Milford, it signifies the end. Very few people in need of palliative care come home from Milford in better shape than they went in. Actually, very few come home at all. When we suggested to Dad that he go to Milford, he rejected it out of hand. As far as he was concerned, he was going to beat the cancer and get back to life on his own terms. The only place he was going was Moyross, to his own bed, and God help anyone that was trying to stop him. Logically and medically, this was the wrong move, but secretly I was delighted. I loved his spirit, his fight and his will to live. What a man! I spent a lifetime arguing with my dad, at times not really liking him, being frustrated by him, breaking his heart and bank balance, but when I was taking him home, I looked at him in the passenger seat and I was never prouder of him. I never loved him more than I did at that time.

Dad's time at home was short-lived. The public health nurse called regularly, as did his GP, Ray O'Connor. We installed a stairlift, and his friends called to see him, but he was getting weaker and weaker. He needed full-time palliative care. It was too hard on Mam, and it was taking a toll on her. My sister Niamh made the call to Milford, and arrangements were made. The end was nigh.

September brought the last bit of joy that Dad had in his life, and it involved his first true love and ardent passion: Clare hurling. Dad was born in 1945 in Newmarket-on-Fergus, the first of six children born to Paddy Sheedy (whom I was named after) and his wife Anna. The family home was a mere stone's throw from where our current president, Michael D. Higgins, was reared. As a child in the 1950s, Dad spent a long time in a hospital in Foynes, County Limerick, as a result of contracting tuberculosis, a disease that was rife in Ireland at that time. When he was in his mid-teens he dropped out of school and went to look for work in the nearby Shannon Industrial Estate. He got taken on in a textiles factory called Lana-Knit, and it was there that he met a diminutive, fiery girl from Limerick called Pearl Hickey.

Dad loved hurling more than anything else in the whole world. I can count on one hand the number of Clare championship matches we missed. In 2013, Clare had managed to climb to the summit again and reach the final, where they would play Cork. Since we couldn't attend the match in person, we watched it at home in Moyross, the staff in Milford having allowed me to take him home for the occasion. The final was a classic, with Clare getting a last-gasp equaliser to force a replay. The excitement of the game nearly killed Dad. He always got excited at games. Watching him struggle to cheer on his beloved team was heartbreaking.

The replay took place a week later, and Clare won in a canter. Dad came home again to watch it, and although he was extremely frail and under the influence of lots of really strong medication, the smile on his face was a joyous thing to behold. Then, when we got back to Milford that evening, something happened that caused uproarious laughter for both of us. I have a cousin, Dan, who is Uncle Tommy's son. Dan is one funny fucker. There's no other way to describe him, and Dad was very fond of him. Dan, in turn loved Dad and regularly visited him in Milford, as he lived nearby. In true Sheedy fashion, Dan was also a passionate Clare hurling supporter. When we arrived back at Dad's room, I opened the door wide to wheel him in. There was a lumpy, crumpled Clare flag draped across the whole bed. I presumed one of the staff must have left it there for Dad to celebrate the win. He was delighted to see it. I went to take the flag off and put him to bed, when the flag started moving. I pulled it off the bed to find Dan underneath, decked out in a Clare jersey, reeking of beer, snoring like a truck and beaming like a kipper! Dad was literally crying, he laughed so much. It was to be the last time I really saw him laugh and be truly happy. I'm just as fond of Dan as Dad was, and I'll never forget the joy he brought to us that day by his drunken visit. I'll always be grateful to him for providing it.

CHAPTER 28

There was something wrong. With me. Not physically, but mentally. I was starting to redevelop all of my insecurities. I was paranoid for no reason. I was looking nervously at police cars again despite the fact that I had been an absolute saint for the past three and a half years. I was convinced that Fiona was going to dump me because I was so overweight and not good enough for her. I was constantly stressed because of Dad's situation. Every time I visited him, I was left wondering if that was going to be the last time I spoke to him. And I was very worried about how Mam was dealing with it all. She never showed any emotion and was convinced that this cancer was just a temporary thing. I knew that this was her way of dealing with it, but I couldn't understand it.

Looking back now, it's pretty clear that this was the beginning of my big implosion. It would take a while to manifest itself into full-blown gambling addiction again, but the wheels were definitely in motion. Fiona was the first to catch on to this. At this stage, she had been in recovery herself for 16 years, and she knew the addiction playbook off by heart. 'You can't kid a kidder.'

My new boss wanted me to go on an induction course in Dublin for two weeks. I had mixed feelings about this. Dad was in serious decline. He was permanently bed-bound and completely out of it most of the time due to the massive amounts of morphine he was on. I didn't want to leave him. I didn't want to be away from Fiona, either, as I felt she was slipping away from me – two weeks apart would, in my mind, increase the divide I felt existed. But it was too good a job, so I packed a bag and headed off to the Big Smoke on a Monday morning.

The first week went well. The hotel was at Newlands Cross, which was ideal for me as I was travelling on the M7. It was of the budget variety, but quite nice – exactly what I'd expect from the Limerick man who owned it. The lads on the induction course were A1. We were all around the same age and from different parts of the country, so there was lots of banter about sport. When I came home on the Friday, I called straight into Milford, as it's on the way into Limerick from the Dublin Road. I knew what to expect, as I had been on the phone hourly, every day, to whichever family member was with Dad or to the nursing staff. He was unrecognisable from the man he was. He was now a shell, but thanks to the amazing care he was receiving from the staff and the copious amounts of medication he was taking, he was relatively pain-free and oblivious to all that was going on around him.

Mam was doing her usual thing: blocking everything out and pretending nothing was wrong. I'm the gambler in the family, and history dictates that I am a pretty bad one; but if this woman learned to play poker, she'd be unreadable. The next few years would reveal to me how deeply she felt about Dad, and how broken she really was by all of this. But for now, she was dealing with it in her own way, and all we could do was be there for her.

I got to Ennis late that night, and I literally collapsed on to the couch. Fiona made coffee, and we chatted, but my mind was elsewhere. The weekend was spent in Milford and driving Mam around to where she needed to go. She loves the big retail parks, and there's one in Limerick she is crazy about, so I dropped her off there and went home to Moyross for a couple of hours' downtime. I spent the downtime fielding and returning a plethora of phone calls from all and sundry: my friends, my friends in recovery, my counsellors, my neighbours and Dad's friends. The outpour of concern was truly humbling. The man was so respected and loved. To this day, I hate that I could not see the reasons why until much later in both our lives.

The rest of the weekend was spent in familiar fashion. I stayed in the family room in Milford on the Saturday night, and on Sunday night I managed to sneak into Patsy's for a couple of badly needed pints. For the couple of hours I was in the pub, I was inundated with well wishes and people being sympathetic. It was hard not to just get up and go home – all I wanted was to have some quiet time – but this was Dad's local, too, and it was his before it was mine. His friends were my friends, and I loved it that they cared so much, about both of us. My friends Ber and Richie picked up on my mood and suggested we slip away to a pub where we wouldn't be the centre of attention. It was just what I needed.

I was on the road early on Monday morning and got to the induction with time to spare. The next three days were the same as the previous week. I went to bed every night around ten o'clock, and Wednesday night was no different. I was roused by my phone ringing. The digital clock on the stand told me it was 1.10 a.m. I didn't even have to look at the caller display. I knew it would say 'Niamh', and she'd be telling me to get home as there wasn't long left. I put the call on speaker, so I could hurriedly get dressed while she relayed the news.

I was on the road by 1.25 a.m. and walked into Dad's room at 3.15 a.m., the lack of traffic at that time of the morning a blessing. I couldn't see him at first. Aunt Mary and Uncle Tommy, soon to be the last two of six siblings, were sat at the end of the bed, Mam was sitting silently to one side, and my sisters Lisa and Niamh were seated either side of him, each holding his hand and gently talking to him. Dan was pacing the floor. Tommy was first to react to my arrival, walking up to me in floods of tears. He hugged me and whispered in my ear, 'He's nearly gone, Pa.'

Then the priest arrived, and he administered the last rites just after 3.30. I then sat with Dad and held his hand. I told him I was sorry for how I had treated him during his life and that I'd see him again one day. At 4.25 a.m. on Thursday 31 October 2013, the man whom I had spent a lifetime loving and letting down drew his last breath.

After the nurses explained to us the next steps, I went to the chapel in Milford. As a kid, I had always had great faith. I was God-fearing, and I regularly attended mass. I had even given genuine thought to becoming a priest shortly after making my confirmation. My faith was yet another thing that gambling took from me, though I'm delighted to be getting in touch with it again today.

I made some calls to people who needed to know: Dad's friends, my friends and neighbours. The one person I really wanted to call, *needed* to call, was Fiona. But I couldn't. I had spoken to her the night before, and she was due to travel to Maynooth University that morning with her daughter, who was receiving her master's degree. If I had told Fiona that Dad was gone, she wouldn't have travelled to Maynooth, and her daughter wouldn't have wanted to either. So I didn't call her, and when she had called me during the day, I pretended that nothing had happened.

I brought Mam into Griffin's undertakers that morning. She wanted to make the arrangements and, since there were no logistical reasons not to, she also wanted to have the service immediately. She picked an absolutely beautiful coffin. I know it might seem odd to describe a coffin as 'beautiful', but it really was. The next evening, Dad would be removed from the funeral home to the church in Moyross, and the mass would be at 10 a.m. on the Saturday.

A few months earlier, I had had a frank conversation with my dad about where he wanted to be buried. He was 1,000 per cent a Newmarket-on-Fergus man, and his parents and brother were buried in an idyllic cemetery overlooking Fenloe Lake. If to be buried there was his wish, then I was going to make it happen, even though I'd probably incur the wrath of Mam and maybe my sisters. But then he told me something that I found remarkable. He said that he had moved to Limerick when he was 21. He was now 68, and by his math that meant he had lived in Limerick a hell of a lot longer than in Clare. He then laughed and said: 'Pearl will fucking kill you if you make her go to Newmarket for a funeral.' He was right. She wouldn't have been impressed, and I'm glad he took a difficult situation out of my hands.

After the undertaker's, I went home with Mam. Her sister arrived, and both my sisters were also there, as were Mam's friends. It was now lunchtime. I didn't fancy being stuck in the middle of that hen party, but I didn't fancy meeting people who were going to be consoling me all day either. I knew where I was going to go.

I arrived at Fiona's parents' house around half past one. I told her mother what had happened, and she was very decent about the whole thing. I suggested to her that I'd wait there for Fiona to get back, and that if she wanted to go shopping, I'd be happy to sit with Mike, Fiona's dad. Thankfully, she agreed, and ten minutes later it was just him and me and the lunchtime news.

I was very fond of Mike for many reasons, not least his ability to call it like it is, and to do so in a decent way. He looked across at me from his spot on the sofa.

'So, he's gone, is he?'

'He is, Mike. Passed this morning at half four.'

'God love him, poor cratur. He's happy now. Jaysus, but Munster were shockin' last week, weren't they?'

And there it was. The perfect way to sympathise with me. For the next three hours, Mike and I listened to old music from when he was a fiddler in the Kilfenora Céilí Band, talked about rugby and argued about the best way to eat spare ribs. He insisted with cabbage; I was more of a turnip guy.

At half four I looked out the window and saw Fiona's car on the way up the drive.

She immediately ran over and hugged me for what seemed like an eternity. And it was just what I needed. I asked her who had told her, but she said that nobody had. She had known the moment she saw my car in her parents' driveway. We went home, grabbing an Indian takeaway on the way. At nine o'clock, I headed for my real home to spend some time with Mam, and to get ready for what was going to be a tough couple of days.

CHAPTER 29

The next day was the longest day of my life. The removal wasn't until 5.30 p.m. and due to leave the undertaker's at 7 p.m. We were invited in at three o'clock to spend some time with Dad as a family before the sympathisers came. I was up with the birds, as I couldn't sleep, so I readied Dad's best suit, shirt and tie for the undertaker. At ten o'clock I brought them in to him. I thanked him for everything and told him we'd see him later.

At 3 p.m., my sisters, their husbands and kids met Mam and me at the funeral home. Dad looked so handsome and peaceful. The undertaker had done a great job of making him look as presentable as he would have made himself were he going to a wedding. Our parish priest arrived, and we said the rosary and some other prayers. At 4 p.m. the other family members arrived: Dad's brother and sister, nieces and nephews, Mam's sister. Little mementos were placed in the coffin: Dan put a Manchester United scarf, and there was a match programme from Clare's recent win in the All-Ireland, a Shannon RFC scarf and a Sharon Shannon CD. I had written a long letter to him, trying to explain my fuck-up of a life and why I was such a bad son. But I also told him how much I loved him and appreciated him. I put that letter in the inside pocket of his suit. It would go to the grave with him.

At 5.10 p.m., Gerry Griffin, the undertaker, told me that there was an 'unexpectedly large crowd' gathering outside and, given the location of the funeral home, it could cause traffic problems. Would we mind if he opened the doors a little earlier? I said that this was fine, then I walked to the door and was totally blown away by the crowds that had amassed to pay their respects. I went back inside, and we took our places: the men standing guard in a line by the door, and the women seated opposite the coffin.

The removal, scheduled for 90 minutes, took two hours and twenty. I was reacquainted with people I hadn't seen in years. My sisters had huge support from their friends, as did my mother. I, too, was taken aback by the amount of people who came to sympathise with me, especially from the recovery community. Friends from GA in Dublin, Galway, Cork and even as far away as Sligo came to pay their respects. Practically the whole village of Newmarket-on-Fergus arrived, as did Dad's ex-colleagues from the places he had worked: Wang, Burlington and Analog. There were four boxes filled with condolence cards, hundreds in each one.

The cortège arrived at the church just after eight. The church in Moyross is very small, and a huge crowd had already congregated. The brief service over, we all went home. The house was crowded with friends of Mam and my sisters. I slipped away into town and Patsy's. It was where Dad would want me to be.

The mass was at ten o'clock the next morning. I had breakfast with Mam and got down to the church around a quarter to. There was already a sizeable crowd, with cars parked all over the estate. I got a little laugh out of this. There were a lot of people here who would never have come within an ass's roar of Moyross. Now they were having to park their cars a few hundred metres away from the church, in the middle of an estate with one of the worst reputations in Ireland. I'm sure Dad got a laugh too. He was very proud of being from Moyross.

By 10 a.m., the church was jam-packed, and the grounds were also crammed. I was doing the eulogy, apparently. Given my flair for talking shite and telling a good story, I suppose I was the obvious candidate. But the truth is that I had forgotten all about it. I had prepared nothing. And to make matters worse, the priest asked for the eulogy to be given at the start of the service, and not near the end, as it had been at every other funeral mass I had ever attended. I nervously made my way to the pulpit.

I don't know how long I spoke for. I mentioned how Mam and Dad met, how they loved and tolerated each other in equal measure. I spoke about the things he was most ardent about: his grandchildren, especially Katie; Clare hurling, Manchester United, Shannon and Munster Rugby; and travelling. Among the attendants there were tears, there was laughter and, at the end, a long round of applause. I had winged it but got away with it. I was so relieved. The thing about giving a eulogy is that even if I made a balls of it, and I may well have done, nobody was ever going to say so, and everybody was going to applaud out of respect, anyway. It was win-win under very sad circumstances.

After mass, we made our way to Mount St Lawrence cemetery, where Dad would be laid to rest. The family plot sees him eternally rest beside his father-in-law, Jim Hickey. Jim and Dad really liked each other, sharing similar passions for Clare hurling and good Guinness. Aunt Angela's husband Tom is also there (he passed away six months before Dad), as is Katie's brother David, whom I spoke about earlier. Again, there was a large congregation in attendance, and I'll never forget the numbness I felt embracing Mam and my sisters as Dad went to his final resting place.

The social etiquette of the day after funerals involved a lavish feast in a swanky hotel for family and friends. We didn't go for this, but not because it was a waste of good money. We decided that the ideal place for it would be somewhere everybody would feel comfortable – and where better than Dad's favourite watering hole? I rang Patsy's at short notice, and they laid out a super spread of buffet-style food that everyone could enjoy while having a few decent pints. I took a quick spin home to ditch the car, and in the process I ditched the black suit also. I donned my favourite jeans and a polo shirt, and I headed for Patsy's to see Dad off in style.

CHAPTER 30

My life was about to enter a crucial phase, and what happened next was a series of events that would plunge me into the depths of depression, self-destruction and ravenous addiction.

The first thing to fall apart was my relationship. I couldn't shake the paranoia and the feelings of not being good enough for Fiona. I had started to buy her gifts she didn't need, or maybe even want. I'd send her flowers, buy things for the house that I thought she'd like and take her out to fancy restaurants. But really, she seemed happier if I bought her a takeaway and a packet of her favourite cigarettes.

I was going out of my way to help her daughter get work experience that could help her career. I organised an internship that backfired. It backfired because I told Fiona's daughter that she was going to get paid a small fee for it. She wasn't going to be, but I was lodging money anonymously to her bank account out of my own pocket. When this stopped because I wasn't able to afford it, Fiona rang the company wanting to know why there were no wages. The whole thing unravelled, and I spiralled into a web of lies trying to cover it up.

At the same time, I started to question Fiona's commitment to me. I felt that she wasn't giving me the reassurances that I felt I deserved and that I definitely needed, given my lack of self-esteem. One day I asked her to meet me for lunch. I had a sneaky feeling that she didn't want it to be known publicly in the town that we were an item. She said she was busy but would see me later at home. I was near her workplace, and at lunchtime I saw her go into the pub next door with a male colleague. I went in, she saw me and nearly hid under the table. *Why wouldn't she go to lunch with me? Was she ashamed of me?* Let's face it, I was a morbidly obese, average-looking guy. She could do much better than me. Or that's how my mind was working, anyway. She gave me an excuse about getting some unexpected free time and going for a quick coffee with this guy. Maybe that was the truth? But my paranoia was telling me something else.

The final straw came one evening a week before Christmas. I had gone out to get some dinner. In the time I was gone, a guy that I had do some work on her brother's car called to the house looking for payment. It was only €150, but I didn't have it. I had been putting him on the long finger and never in a million years did I think he'd call to Fiona's house. But call he did, and he told her about how long he'd been waiting to get paid, the number of times I had promised to pay him over the three or so weeks I owed him, and how unreliable and dodgy he thought I was. Fiona was mortified, and her daughter quite upset.

When I got back, I could tell something was up. She came straight out with it – how he had called to her door and what he had told her. About a year later, she would tell me that if I had been honest with her at that time, maybe we could have worked through it. But I wasn't, and the more she asked me to be, the more I tried to bullshit my way out of it and deflect the blame elsewhere. I told her I was about to get a really big break with a job, and that I'd love to take her to New York on a shopping trip. Eventually, she told me to go. As I said earlier, trying to fool her was a ridiculous thing to do, and I don't know how I thought it was going to work. But the addict's brain was already back at work, even though I kept telling myself it wasn't.

Next morning, I got a text from Fiona. I was full of hope: hope that she might forgive me, that she might pity me and help me. Hope that it wasn't all over. The text was short and brutal: 'Meet ****** outside Spar shop at eleven to collect your things. Give her your house keys. Don't call me.' That was that. She wanted no more to do with me. If I had been gored by a raging bull, I wouldn't have felt any worse than I did at that point.

I got home at lunchtime, and I took the big suitcase into which I had crammed my possessions up to my bedroom. I threw it on the bed, and I just sat there, almost afraid to unpack it. I heard a noise and turned around. There, at the door, was Mam. She shook her head and asked me what I did to warrant getting thrown out and dumped. I lied and told her that nothing was wrong. Just like with Fiona, there was no point in lying to this woman. She had lived a lifetime with my lies, my bullshit and my addictive habits. She certainly wasn't going to believe me this time, either.

Christmas 2013 was the worst on record. It was my first Christmas in 44 years without Dad, my first Christmas in 20 years not taking him to one of the local sports clubs for a pint before dinner. These clubs had a special licence to operate on Christmas morning, and they were very popular. Many a blazing row was had in homes across Limerick City on Christmas Day because Johnny or Jimmy had come home drunk from the club for the big dinner. And it happened in our house, too. I'd get the blame because I took him, and I should have known better.

I had planned to wake up that morning with Fiona, exchanging gifts before taking Dad up to the Fairview Club, then home for dinner and a lazy day. My plans didn't exactly work out that year. I woke up alone, in the small box room I had grown up in, and I had no dad to bring for a pint. I didn't even bother getting dressed, and I spent the day being a miserable moaner, wallowing in self-pity.

St Stephen's Day. A huge day in the gambling world. While I wouldn't actually gamble, I was already gambling in my mind. My self-esteem was shot to pieces, and true to form (pardon the pun), I began to think (again) that the only way to restore it was through popularity and money. I went to the pub with the lads and watched everyone around me enjoying the buzz of having a few bets with the few pints. I resisted the urge that day, and I did so for quite a while. But I was the equivalent of a 'dry drunk', an alcoholic who behaves as if he was drinking even when he is not. My gambling persona was slowly but surely on the way back. And truth be told, I was looking forward to it coming back. Because yet again, and just as I had been in 2003, I was full of arrogance and self-belief. I believed that this time I wouldn't make the same mistakes, that I would be the one in control. I spent the next eight months fighting with myself. But by August 2014 I had finally fallen on my sword, an ever-sharpening sword and one that I kept falling on for the next six years.

By mid-2014, I was well and truly on the road to a full-blown collapse. There was no gambling – yet– but the 'stinking thinking' was there, and my self-esteem was plummeting. In a desperate attempt to win Fiona back, I decided to go on one of those miracle diets that were all the fashion at the time. I read about it online but nearly had a stroke when I saw how much it cost. You had to buy your food from the company who prescribed the diet, and it would have cost up to €100 a week if it was to be done correctly. What I did next was the first sign that I was slipping back into my old ways.

I called up the company and pretended to be doing a customer service review of the best diets for seriously overweight people. They bought it, hook, line and sinker. Every week for the next three months, I went to their local office, collected my food pack and got weighed and assessed, paying for none of it. I also joined a gym, and between the diet and the exercise, I lost somewhere in the region of 70lb. Fiona seemed impressed, and so did a lot of other people who commented on how well I looked. I felt better too. Then, on the run-up to Dad's first anniversary, Fiona made it clear that there would be no going back. It was over with a capital O. Within three months, I was back to – and soon exceeding – my pre-diet weight, comfort-eating like an elephant and drowning my sorrows, too.

Deep down, I knew there was no going back with Fiona. But I just didn't want to let go. She was the first woman that I really saw myself spending the rest of my life with, and it hurt for years afterwards. I have been able to look back on that whole experience with hindsight, and I can now see that she may not have been the perfect woman I had thought she was. But I was the one that put her up on a pedestal. I was the one that did all the running, and I allowed myself to get caught up in the romance of it all, allowed myself to dream of a fairy-tale ending. Without being too cynical, fairy tales are read by doting parents to their infants before bedtime – they don't exist in the real world. I learned a painful lesson with Fiona. But I'm pretty sure it will prove to be a valuable one, and if the opportunity for romance comes knocking again, I'll have a more pragmatic view of it. That's for sure.

CHAPTER 31

ife went into free fall pretty quickly after Fiona and I broke up. I was lost. I had invested everything in that relationship, and I really had thought that it was *the* one. When it ended, I was too proud to admit to my friends that it had all gone south. As far as I could tell, they were all of the impression that I was totally 'loved up' and had been building a new life for myself. I was, of course, wrong. As the weeks and months went by, I started to appear more and more in the pub or at gatherings when I normally would be with Fiona. The lads did as they normally would, pretending they knew of nothing wrong. But I was as transparent as clear glass. When I finally plucked up the courage to tell them, it came as no surprise that they already knew. Again, they proved themselves to be nothing short of absolute diamonds, and they supported me, listening to me whinge and moan and telling me to 'cop the fuck on' when I needed to be told.

The first scam that would see me go to prison for anything longer than a few days came about at this time. In 2010, I had befriended a guy called Keith in Bushy Park, and I went on to work as a facilitator with him. We would go to matches and meetings together, and he was a pretty cool guy, a little egotistical but with good reason: he was a good-looking man, and he knew it. He worked as a freelance landscape gardener and one day made the cardinal mistake of telling me that he was in the market for some equipment. Although not gambling yet, I was on the verge of doing so, and I saw an opportunity here: I could scam some of the equipment he needed from whatever company sold it, and only charge him a fraction of the price. *Everyone's a winner*, I thought. It was an opportunity for me to fund the gambling spree I had been subconsciously planning for a while now. I also needed money to start being a Flash Harry again. I needed a new wardrobe, and to start rebuilding the persona of a successful man about town.

Keith was suitably impressed when I told him I could get the equipment at half the price. Without hesitation, he transferred the money to me, and the merry-go-round started to spin. Then the problems began. I had serious difficulty in convincing the company to give me the goods on credit as I had presumed they would. I tried several strokes under several guises over the next few weeks, but to no avail. Maybe I was losing my touch.

I wasn't quite sure what to do next, and desperation started to kick in. Being a recovering addict himself, Keith soon began to smell the bullshit. I relied on the usual excuses to buy more time. He regularly called and told me that he was under pressure from his dad, who was good friends with a chief superintendent, that he had no choice but to go to the guards, but that he wouldn't do so if I repaid him the money. I repaid him what I could, when I could; eventually, almost a year later, I had repaid him all I owed him. I felt a great sense of relief and pride. Repaying Keith meant not only that he wouldn't report me to the gardaí, but also that I did the right thing by him. That relief was short-lived.

At this stage I was gambling again. My recollections of my first bet this time aren't as clear, mostly because I was in the throes of depression. I was mentally destroyed. I remember opening a betting account with BoyleSports and Bet365. I was barred from Paddy Power over the voucher scam, and Ladbrokes had decided to exclude me. This was actually very responsible of them, and looking back, I appreciate it. They reviewed my history and made the decision to exclude me based on that. But I was also very aware that I didn't want anyone seeing me walk into a bookies, so I did all my gambling the most dangerous way I could: online.

I was at home one morning when an unmarked squad car pulled up outside the door. I automatically felt sick. The detective, who introduced himself as being from Ennis Garda Station, said that he'd appreciate it if I'd accompany him to the station to answer some questions regarding a complaint made by Keith.

The garda asked me if it would be more comfortable to have the interview in Shannon Garda Station since I knew a few officers in the Ennis station personally.

I met the detectives in Shannon, as agreed, a few days later. I wasn't arrested or cautioned. I still thought – or hoped against hope, more like – that Keith would withdraw the charges, seeing as I had repaid him in full. During the interview I gave away very little, and I was released without charge a couple of hours later. I heard nothing for a few weeks, which gave me hope that Keith had reconsidered. False hope. The next time the detectives knocked at my door, it would be to arrest me. This time, there was no point in trying to dance the dance with them. They had all their ducks in a row, and I was well and truly screwed.

I was charged in October 2016 with deception and 'using a false instrument', a charge for making up a bogus invoice, and sentenced to 15 months. The judge called me some pretty offensive, if accurate, names, including 'master of deception' and 'career criminal'. I was brought to Ennis Garda Station and then to Limerick Prison. I lodged an immediate appeal, but an independent surety had to be paid, and that involved getting my solicitor to call my mother. The wheel had turned full circle, yet again, but this time I could really sense her weariness of me and the life I seemed to constantly choose. I spent one night in Limerick Prison on remand, then Mam came up to pay my bail, and I was free pending appeal. She didn't speak to me on the walk back into town, or for a few days afterwards.

A few days later, I was on my way to gamble my social welfare money after collecting it from the post office when I heard a sudden 'pop'. Next thing I knew, I was on the ground and couldn't get up. I had snapped my Achilles tendon clean in two. In layman's terms, my foot was no longer connected to my lower leg. There was a simple reason this happened: I was morbidly obese, and the joints and tendons in my body were under enormous pressure. Strangely, I wasn't in too much pain, but I could not stand on my own two feet. I got a taxi to A&E, where they didn't even need to X-ray my leg. They knew simply by looking at it. They put it in a protective boot that enabled me to stand with the aid of crutches. I was referred to an orthopaedic surgeon and sent home.

The following week, I got a call from the hospital telling me to report for surgery. It was the only way to fix it. I packed an overnight bag and went to University Hospital Limerick. I had a scare during surgery. Because of my weight, the anaesthetist had to administer large amounts of anaesthetic when giving me my epidural. My blood pressure plummeted, and there was a lot of panicked conversation going on in theatre. Eventually, they managed to sort everything out, and the operation was a success. I had to stay in hospital for two weeks in recovery, largely again due to my weight and the complications it brought.

CHAPTER 32

Christmas sucked. I was in a protective boot and plaster cast, and the recovery was going to take up to a year. I was broke, depressed and now immobile. Life really was shit, and about to get worse. I got a letter from my solicitor early in the New Year advising me that my appeal was up on 31 January. Past experiences of my appeals against prison sentences were all good. I told myself that this would be no different. And now I was on crutches with a bad injury, what judge wouldn't take pity on me?

The answer to that question is Judge Francis Comerford. He reviewed my history, my circumstances and the crime I was sentenced for (deception and using a false instrument). He decided that I was going to prison – end of. But thankfully not for the 15 months. He reduced the sentence to five months. I looked up to the gallery where the gardaí sit in court and saw a garda I was friendly with. I often socialised with him. He actually had to excuse himself from investigating this case because he knew me. The arresting detective was his partner. I saw this garda shake his head in disgust when the judge said he was reducing my sentence. This was almost as hurtful as having to go to jail.

The judge gave me a week to get my affairs in order. I went home and told Mam. She took the news as I expected her to: with a silent shrug of her shoulders and expressions of her disappointment in me. My buddy Pat drove me up to the prison a week later, and my first prison sentence began. I wasn't to stay in Limerick, however. The fact that I was on crutches and couldn't climb stairs created huge accessibility problems, so I was transferred to Cork Prison, where there was a ground-floor landing that could accommodate me. I was brought down in a taxi as I couldn't climb the steps to get into the prison van.

Prison wasn't what I had expected it to be. Because of my injury, my experience of it didn't reflect real prison. I was confined to my cell all of the time due to my injury, and I didn't really mix with anyone other than the lads I met when I went to the yard once a day for fresh air and exercise. Because it was a first-time sentence (and considered a short one), my stay in prison was relatively brief. A governor came to my cell one morning and told me to pack my bag: I was going home. My first real prison experience lasted five weeks. I got taken by taxi to the bus station and given a voucher for a one-way ticket home. It all felt surreal. I would have to go to a probation service every week for the remainder of the sentence, but the whole thing passed very quickly.

My next problem was learning how to live with my new-found persona non grata status. Word spread that I had been in prison, and I was the subject of a pretty vindictive social-media campaign. I actually had to go to the gardaí about it. A guy I knew through Facebook read about my prison stint in the local paper. He started a thread that went viral, and within a very short space of time it was causing me huge problems. The guy posted a picture of me, along with my address, which meant that my mother's address was now attached to this viral thread. This was bad enough. Shortly after this, one particular smart-ass keyboard warrior whom I had never even met decided to put up a post suggesting that 'a gang get together, go to his house and beat some manners into the fat scumbag prick'. I've never been violent in my life. Ever. But right there and then, my first instinct was to go after this guy and put some manners of my own on him. I didn't fear this guy or any of his friends, but when a Facebook thread goes viral, it really goes viral. I didn't know what kind of people were reading this, and what kind of danger I could be in as a result. After speaking to my probation officer and my sister (who was a great help through all of this), I decided that my best option was to report it as a threat to the gardaí.

I had been reluctant to do this for many reasons. Part of me felt that I deserved to be treated like this, that I really *was* a scumbag and long overdue a good kicking. Part of me felt that the people who posted these things weren't really bad people, they were just reacting to my appalling behaviour. But another part of me felt like a victim of a crime; I was also a little afraid that, as a result of this threat, the wrong kind of people could come knocking on my door and my mother could suffer. I emailed the guys involved – the originator of the thread and the guy who had put up the threat – and asked for the whole thing to be taken down. They laughed at me and posted that I was on to them begging for mercy and pity. I immediately went to Mayorstone Park Garda Station and made a statement.

The gardaí didn't have much sympathy for me and tried to make light of it. I told them that I expected this complaint to be treated the same way any complaint they ever received about me was. They contacted both guys and told them that they should remove the entire thread at once, which they did. I let the matter drop at that. Nobody had anything to gain from it.

Life was as bad as it ever was right then, and sadly not destined to get any better for a long, long time. In April 2016, I was arrested in connection with the charges I was sentenced to time in prison for in 2020. These charges were for obtaining money by false pretences, namely getting money from people who were told that I would be supplying them with Rugby World Cup tickets the previous year.

This matter would be dealt with in the Circuit Court, so I knew that I would receive a sentence of at least two years, probably more. What I didn't foresee was the length of time it would take to get matters finalised.

A problem arose when I was being arraigned, and details of my previous convictions were read out in open court. I nearly fell off the bench reserved for defendants when I heard the state prosecutor read them aloud. They included armed robbery and impersonation of a member of An Garda Síochána. At first, I started laughing. I genuinely thought it was a joke. I called my barrister over and told him that these previous convictions were completely fictitious. The judge ordered a review and remanded me on bail. It would take over a year for the state to put together the correct list of my previous convictions. The delays continued.

Unfortunately, the judge got seriously ill and needed to take a long time off. This delayed things by another year. I wasn't complaining. I didn't want the matters dealt with, although with hindsight, I would have been far better off having them dealt with swiftly. When the judge was fit again, I had some health issues of my own, but truth be told, I exaggerated these to try and keep myself out of jail a little longer. In some perverse way, I felt that the longer I put things off, the greater the chance that the problem would just go away. That's typical addict behaviour. The problem certainly wasn't going away.

Then COVID came. More delays, more cancellations. Finally, 14 October 2020 came. I got up at seven. I showered, got dressed and began packing my prison bag. Despite the sense of defeat and inevitability, part of me still clung to the hope that I'd be back home that afternoon. I hugged Mam and told her, for the millionth time in a very troubled life, that I was sorry for everything. I said goodbye to the cat and saw my taxi pull up outside. I looked back at Mam, but I knew another hug or apology would be pointless. I walked out in the rain and told the taxi driver to take me to Mulgrave Street. The next time I'd speak to Mam would be from a prison telephone.

CHAPTER 33

/ 'Should we cuff him?'

'Nah, what's the point? Look at the size of the fat bastard ... he's going nowhere'.

This was the gist of the conversation the two prison escort guards were having about me as they were getting ready to put me into the sweatbox. 'Sweatbox' is a not-so-endearing term for the big prison transport trucks that you often see coming and going from courtrooms and on the news. In my case, the term was more applicable than most. At 28.5 stone in weight and with very poor mobility, I literally had to turn sideways and inhale as deeply as I could to get into the little cramped space where I had to sit. The compartment was a really confined space in which even a person of a normal build would be uncomfortable. Although the journey was literally only 200 yards in distance, it felt like 200 miles (I felt every bump and turn in the road), and eventually I was driven through the gate of Limerick Prison. It was beginning.

I was brought to reception, where I had to strip naked and shower. I was then made to sit on 'The Chair'. This was an X-ray device designed to detect any drugs I might have concealed in my person. The thought that anyone could fill a condom with drugs and insert it up their back passage appalled me. It literally made me cringe. I was then handed my kit bag, which contained a starched white bed sheet and a matching lime-green-and-grey check pillowcase and duvet cover. It also had a well-used but washed pink-orange towel, a cheap toothbrush, a tiny tube of prison-issue toothpaste, sachets of shampoo and a small bar of soap. I was then told that I would be in quarantine for 14 days as part of COVID-19 guidelines. I was brought through to D2 landing, and all that was missing was a 'Welcome to Hell' sign. It was miserable. Guys screaming from their cell doors as I passed: 'What you here for, bud?' and 'Any stuff on ya, sham?' and 'Haha boys, it's the fat c**t from Moyross dat lives in de bookies.'

The officer showed me to my cell, and told me that I'd be called to see the governor in the morning, and that my tea would be delivered at 4 p.m. The first thing I looked for was a television. Thankfully, the bog-standard 20-inch Walker TV was there, fully equipped with some of the finest channels Saorview has to offer. E4 repeats were to become a staple in my life for the next two and a half years. There was no remote, but I wasn't really expecting one. There was also a small kettle, a well-recycled plastic mug, green in colour, with a matching plate, bowl, knife, fork and spoon. In the corner was a stainless-steel toilet that wasn't so stainless, and a sink. I spent my first hour scrubbing the toilet and the sink as best as I could. I soaked the cutlery and dishes and hoped for the best when I had to actually use them. Tea arrived at 4 p.m. My first of over 1,000 prison meals. My culinary delight that evening constituted a brown cardboard box full of beans with two sausages buried in among them. I only picked at it and binned the rest. I didn't even bother using the plate.

Strangely enough, I slept like a log. I think I just accepted the situation pretty quickly. Next morning, I woke early, petrified that I was going to be all over the news. I wasn't, and I was really glad for my family. I knew they all would be hurting, especially my mother, in different ways. A bag of Rice Krispies and a pint of milk was thrown in the door to me at eight. I washed at the sink and made a cup of tea, which was vile. I think it was a combination of poor water quality and yellow-pack teabags. I turned on the telly and watched *Ireland AM*. At ten, I was summoned to meet the governor.

I went to his office at the end of the landing. There was nobody out because of COVID, just officers and a prisoner who was cleaning the landing. He gave me the once-over, no doubt picking up on my nervousness, embarrassment and general feeling of not belonging here. To the officers I was a novelty. I could speak eloquently. I was respectful. I wasn't threatening them or trying to be something I wasn't. But I still got a bad vibe from them, and I felt that if I said or did the slightest wrong thing, the living shit would be kicked out of me quicker than I could blink. The governor was very matter-of-fact. He got me to confirm my name, address and next of kin, and he read me the court warrant explaining the reasons for my incarceration. He told me that I would be quarantined in accordance with HSE COVID guidelines for two weeks and then be moved to C wing, and that I would be seen by a doctor. And that was that. Back to Cell 6, D2 landing.

Later that morning, I heard the door opening. An officer I had known quite well for years came in to check on me. He went away and came back armed with a remote control (pure gold in prison circles in Limerick), extra toiletries and some books and newspapers. He also took my sister's phone number and promised to check in with her regularly. This was a big comfort to me. I was delighted to see a friendly face and to get the extra goodies, especially the remote. Also, I knew he'd put the word around to other officers that I wasn't the worst, which added an extra layer of protection. However, he also warned me of the dangers of telling any other prisoners that we knew each other. That could be very detrimental to both of us.

The next 13 days were like Groundhog Day, every single one of them. Boring, monotonous, routine. No fresh air or exercise was beginning to take its toll. I washed at the sink in the cell because the shower block was absolutely rancid. It was as if the world had stood still. Then, on 27 October, at 10 a.m., I was told to pack my kit. I was going over to C2 landing. I was entering the big time. I guess my buddy was able to pull a small string for me, because I was given my own cell. This was massive for me. I really don't think I was capable of doubling up. I made my bed and sorted out my few bits and bobs. Then I went through the ritual of scrubbing a toilet and sink for an hour all over again.

I felt like I was the new arrival at the zoo. Everyone on the landing converged at my door. Some of them to get a look at me, some to see if I had brought any goodies with me, either of the chocolate or narcotic variety. I knew a couple of them, including a guy who had played football in a club I was involved with. He was in for extortion, loan sharking and intimidation. He assured me that I'd be okay and if I needed anything to come to him. I also saw some neighbours, kids who grew up round Moyross. Most of them didn't know me, partly because I had been living in Dublin when they were growing up, partly because I was old enough to be their father and partly because I simply didn't operate in their world, a world that involved drugs, violence and feuding. Looking at their interactions on the landing and the yard, it finally hit me: *I'm one of them now, and this is going to be my life going forward.* Of course, deep down I knew I'd be able to adapt to it. I had been adapting to situations all my life. This was just another chapter in the life of a chameleon. But it was starting to dawn on me that there'd be no more gambling, no more going to matches, no more social life and no more freedom. My ability to take a shower when I wanted was gone. So too was my being able to walk to the shop to get a newspaper, or phone my friends whenever I wanted or needed to. What the fuck had I done?

Prison routine is very strict. You get your door opened at 8.15 a.m. for breakfast, which consists of a bag of cornflakes, Rice Krispies or Weetabix. There's porridge available if you're at the head of the queue. Once you've collected this, it's straight back to your cell until the doors open at 9.20 a.m. There's usually a flurry of interaction when the doors first open, with guys running to other cells to get 'a bit of dust' (tobacco) or something stronger, if it's available. I grabbed my cornflakes and hobbled back up the stairs to my cell as quickly as I could. At 9.20 you're opened up to clean your cell. You grab the nearest mop and bucket, empty your bin and do whatever business you can until 10 a.m. Limerick Prison has a 'yard or cell' policy. If you weren't a cleaner or kitchen worker, you had to either go to the yard or be locked back in your cell. If you were enrolled in school, you might be called for that, but there were no guarantees. I was neither a cleaner or kitchen worker nor enrolled in school, so I went back to the safety of my cell and steered well clear of the madness of the yard. The yard in most prisons is an experience, but the yard in Limerick is a jungle. I was to experience this 18 months later, but that's another story. Guys do all their business in the yard. It's their office. Deals are made, promises are broken. Guys play cards, Don or Switch, or they might they play handball. 'Straighteners' (fights) are regularly occurring to sort out differences. Shivs are made and distributed. Yes, the yard in prison really is where it all happens.

You're sent back from the yard (or your job or school) at 11.45, and dinner gets served at midday. I spent time in four different prisons, and by and large the food is appalling. But Limerick has two redeeming features: its tuck shop and its food, both of which are the best in the prison system. You get your food at the servery and take it back to your cell. I remember my first Limerick dinner very well. It was a huge turkey breast in breadcrumbs with potatoes and veg. I remember actually enjoying it. Your door opens again at 2.15 p.m. and it's the same thing: yard or cell. This time I decided to go to the yard. If I didn't, the rest of the prisoners would be wondering why I was staying behind again. There's a lot of paranoia in prison, and newcomers are always treated with scepticism and considered 'rats' until they prove themselves or are vouched for.

I went to the yard, and it was an hour and a half of being asked the same questions:

'Well, cuz, whatcha in for?' 'You're from Moyross, aren't ya bud?' 'Bring anythin' in with you, kid?'

I answered them all and played the game. I even approached fellas and asked them the same questions I was being asked. I told them about the scams I pulled. They all found the idea of me being in jail hilarious. I wasn't going to have any problems here. Back in at 4 p.m. – tea time. Same routine, take it to your cell. At 5.30 p.m., doors open: yard or cell. However, depending on what officer is working, you might be allowed to stay out on the landing from 6 until lockdown at 7. This is the time it gets busy. There are four floors to C wing in Limerick. Messages regularly get passed up and down the landings – anything from requests for a bit of dust, to a packet of biscuits, to drugs being enclosed in a piece of paper, put in the bristles of a sweeping brush and passed up to the next floor through the metal grille.

There's a hierarchy in Limerick's C wing. C2 landing is where the new committals and the 'troublesome' prisoners are housed. It's a pretty bad landing: loud, aggressive and full of drugs. C3 is a step up, not as noisy and threatening; and C4 is where the long-term, enhanced and life-sentenced prisoners are. It's by far the best landing in the jail, with no fighting and very little drug taking. As a new committal, I was on C2. Thankfully, on my third day, this was about to change.

I was called to the class office, which is where the officers that work on each landing are based. When I went in, an officer was standing behind the desk where a chief officer was seated. A chief officer is a very senior staff member, and it's rare that they will have any interaction with a prisoner other than for disciplinary or administrative purposes. I was told to sit. He asked me how I was settling in and if I knew any officers personally. I wasn't sure how to answer this, as being honest might put my buddy in an awkward position; there was another officer there I also knew, as I had spent a month in treatment with him ten years previously. I hedged my bets and told the chief that yes, I did know two officers personally, but I refused to name them, citing anonymity being required because I knew them through addiction and recovery groups. This seemed to satisfy him. He then told me to go back to my cell and pack my bags.

I was being moved to Portlaoise Prison for 'operational reasons', a term I later grew to detest. The reality was that I was so morbidly obese and immobile, they were afraid I'd fall down the stairs when going to collect my meals and be in a position to sue the prison service. Portlaoise apparently had a ground floor that would suit me. I went back to my cell, happy that I was being moved from this shithole, but apprehensive because I was being sent to a maximum-security prison that was notorious for housing IRA prisoners and cartel assassins. In my mind, I was a small-time con artist. What the fuck was I being put in with these people for?

I was loaded on to the sweatbox at 3 p.m. There were four others being transferred with me, none of whom I knew. This time, when waiting in reception to get into the van, I had 'the eights slapped on'. The 'eights' are handcuffs – so called because they are shaped as a figure eight. Prisoners hate them because there is no chain link between the cuffs, thereby ensuring that your hands are kept very close together in front of you, and they are often closed very tightly by the officers. I found it very difficult to get up the high step of the van and keep my balance, mostly because of my weight. I literally fell on to the bench in the cramped cubicle and felt the door slam shut.

The journey took about an hour and a half. The other four spent the trip shouting messages to each other and asking me the same old questions I had been asked for the previous two days. When we got to the gate, I was delighted – mostly to be getting out of a space that I could hardly breathe in, and also because the handcuffs were so tight, I could see the marks on my wrists from where they were digging into my skin. My delight began to dissipate in ten-minute increments because we were left waiting at the gate for an hour and a half. I didn't know why then, but now I do. It's just one of the many ways that the screws fuck with your head. The other guys were banging doors, screaming that they needed to go to the toilet, demanding phone calls. The attitude of the officers to this was to more or less say 'fuck you'. Then they went for coffee. Trying to dictate terms to an officer is about as futile as trying to piss into the wind – it just blows back on you and gets you nowhere.

At 6 p.m. we were offloaded from the sweatbox and made to stand in a holding area just behind the gate. Then we were chained together in a long line and walked up to the reception area. I felt like I was in an American prison movie, with a chain gang. I was in awe of the sight of the army on the roof of what I now know to be E wing, the Provisional prisoners' wing. I was then notified that, because of COVID, I'd have to go through another 14-day quarantine period. I couldn't fucking believe it. We went to A5 landing in Portlaoise, and I went through the isolation process all over again.

I noticed a different atmosphere here, especially with the officers. Most of them seemed calmer, less on edge and, in general, simply nicer human beings than those in Limerick. I was brought books from the library, and a daily newspaper was dropped in to me when they were finished with it. I always got the phone at the times I requested it. They always asked me how I was and if I needed anything. This made those 14 days of mind-numbing boredom somewhat easier. The showers were the same as Limerick, though – temperamental and filthy. I washed at the sink rather than use them. I had no interaction with anyone other than the officers who called to the door and my two daily phone calls. One of these was always to my mother, sometimes both. I was deeply ashamed of what I had become and where I had ended up.

My quarantine ended on a Saturday. An officer came over and told me to pack up: I was going to C1 landing. I was somewhat apprehensive about this, but at the same time delighted to be getting out of quarantine. By nature, I'm a sociable person, and I thrive on interaction. I missed not talking to others, even if they were some of the country's most notorious criminals. The officer who walked over to C wing with me was a nice lad, and I would get on very well with him over the next year and a half. He told me not to pay any attention to who I might see on the landing, but that I would recognise them.

'Don't mind some of these fellas, now. You'll have seen a few of them in the *Sunday World*. They keep Nicola Tallant in a job, but don't mind 'em.'

I didn't know how to feel about this, though I would soon find out.

Whenever a new prisoner comes on to the landing, the whole landing come out of the woodwork to get a good gawk. This was no different. As I got down to Cell 13 on C1 landing, two menacing-looking bald lads in their late 30s came straight into my cell.

'Yea, bud … story? This is Mick, and you know who I am, yea?' The truth was I hadn't a clue who he was, but I just nodded.

'I run the bleedin' show round here, yea, and if anyone fucks with you just tell 'em to come and see me. You'll be alright here. Whatcha in for?' I told him, although I could tell he wasn't really listening and was more interested in what I had in my kit bag. He helped himself to a bag of popcorn, or 'poppy', as he called it. He then got up and walked off, followed by his devoutly loyal lapdog Mick.

I ventured out for a stroll up and down the landing. It was a much different place than Limerick. The landing was huge: 33 big single cells, all kitted out with a shower, and a big, bright landing. It felt alright. As I was walking down, a diminutive man, maybe 5 foot 6 inches in height, with a big smile on his face, approached me.

'Welcome to Portlaoise, young man,' he said. 'Do you go to mass?' and he tried to hand me some prayer cards with Our Lady on them. I just looked at him, smiled and walked back to my cell. A Jesus freak was all I needed right then. Thankfully, it was almost lock-up time. I banged my door shut and started to unpack my kit. What an interesting evening. I remember feeling strangely comfortable there, and very glad I was out of Limerick.

Around half an hour later, the officer who had brought me over to

C wing earlier came to my cell. He asked me how I was getting on and if I needed anything. I told him that I was fine and thanked him for checking in on me. As he was going, he asked me how I got on with my new 'friends'. He had seen the two bald guys come into my cell and was keeping an eye on the situation from a distance. He had also seen my interaction with the Jesus freak. I can tell you that when he told me who they were, I didn't have the best night's sleep. The bald 'howya' guy was a gangland criminal; the Jesus freak was none other than the legendary Border Fox, Dessie O'Hare.

I would go on to develop very different relationships with them: I grew to really dislike one of them, while the other really helped me during the early stages of my sentence. We formed a friendship that I could never in a million years have envisioned just a month earlier.

I was a physical mess when I entered prison, but my mental state was also a major concern. My arrogance, fuelled by gambling addiction, led me to believe that I was fine, in control and able to manage whatever aspects of my life I needed to. This couldn't have been further from the truth. The reality was that the gambling had finally destroyed me, and that I was at the lowest ebb ever on 14 October 2020.

Early November saw me catch a break. I had asked to see the addiction counsellor in Portlaoise when I arrived, but I was told that the waiting list was so long, there was a fair chance I'd never get to see her, because I was only doing a three-year sentence. Then, Joe, the chaplain, asked me if I was okay. I don't know why, but I threw in the towel and had a heart-to-heart with him about just how bad things were for me and how mentally fragile I was. He immediately got me an appointment with Noeleen, and from that day on, my mental health got what it had so badly needed.

Noeleen dealt mostly with drug addicts, but she was like no other addiction counsellor I had ever met. She knew from my history that I had done the 12-Step programmes before and that I had nothing to gain from going down that road again. She was interested in looking at the causality, the reasons why, the underlying elements that made me an addict and a conman; most importantly for me, she made me look at life through the eyes of the people and companies I had stolen from, and through the eyes of my friends and my family. I logged dozens of sessions with her over the following 18 months, and I will never be able to thank her enough for the tough love she showed me, for being as brutal with me as I needed her to be and for being as compassionate with me as she was when I needed compassion.

Understanding that I'm not a bad person was a huge step for me. So was developing the ability to see and understand the damage I was doing to those I stole from: to understand that it's not okay to steal from a company just because they have insurance, that I affect someone who expects tickets from me that they've promised to their families or clients.

I was also able to examine relationships I have had, like the ones with Dad and Fiona, and understand why I behaved the way I did. I had an innate craving to be loved and to be all things to all people. Noeleen helped me to rediscover my self-esteem and to be as proud of the good things I've done and will do as much as I'm ashamed of the bad things I have done. I really do believe that an individual is only as strong as their mind. Thanks to Noeleen, I feel that today I am as strong as I've ever been mentally, and far better equipped to deal with whatever life throws at me in the future.

*

It was fascinating to compare the dynamics of Limerick Prison and Portlaoise. Limerick was raw and volatile. Portlaoise was different: there was a constant undercurrent of potential carnage waiting to happen, but it remained well under the surface, as opposed to Limerick, where it was evident 24/7. Prisoners in Limerick were more openly aggressive, towards each other and the screws. In Portlaoise, everyone seemed more content. This is because the regimes were so different. The core regime was the same regarding opening-up and lock-in times, but I was really surprised at the freedom given to prisoners in Portlaoise. For example, when opened up at 9.20 a.m. you were free to roam about the landings and mix with all other prisoners on your landing. At 10 a.m. you had the choice of going to the yard or staying on your landing. There was no lock-up if you weren't working. You could freely walk up to the school on C3 or go to the rec room and play pool. One of the things I really thought made a difference was how you addressed the officers. In Limerick it was 'Mr' or 'Miss'. In Portlaoise, you addressed them by their first name. This made more sense to me from a security point of view, but it also made prisoners feel more on a par with the staff and not under their thumb, as you felt in Limerick. The attitude of the officers was much more laid-back also. They asked you how you were, how your family was doing and so on. Now, don't get me wrong: there were a few absolute animals on the staff there also. But, by and large, Portlaoise was definitely the place to be for me. I settled in very quickly.

When I was young, I was quite religious, even God-fearing. I was a regular at mass, and I went to Christian Brothers schools. When I discovered women, sex and, most importantly, gambling, I left all that behind me. A few days in to my Portlaoise holiday, Dessie O'Hare came in to say hello. Let's say I was slightly intimidated and fearful, considering how I had snubbed his offer of a prayer card upon arrival. I immediately apologised for being rude and started to stutter out an excuse. He looked at me and smiled, then laughed and told me not to worry. For a man in his mid-60s, he has the most impish, childlike smile, and his demeanour totally belies the notorious reputation he has earned. He asked me if I believed in God. I told him that I did, though I had a lot of reasons to doubt Him given how my life had turned out. He then proceeded to tell me his life story. It literally blew me away. There are publishers that would pay him an obscene advance for the rights to publish his story. It's not my story to tell, but what I will say is that Dessie O'Hare, the globally feared and renowned terrorist, is responsible for me rediscovering my faith. I'll never be a devout churchgoer, but I do go to mass regularly now, and I pray in my own way daily. Any man who gets shot over 20 times in one go and lives to tell the tale is entitled to promote the existence of God without fear of contradiction. And let's be honest – who is going to argue with the Border Fox?

The doctor wouldn't clear me for any kind of physical work, given my weight and need of a new hip. So I decided to enrol in the school. Climbing the stairs was a challenge, but I got there and did the interview with Evelyn, the supervising teacher. As I mentioned at the start of this book, my old addiction counsellor had told me that there were the makings of a good book in me. I mentioned this to Evelyn, and she put me down for three classes a week with Shauna, the creative writing teacher. With nothing to lose, and plenty of time on my hands, I decided to give it a go. I did QQI Level 5 courses in both Creative Writing and Research & Study Skills, and a Level 6 in Communications. I loved it. I learned a hell of a lot in a short space of time, and once I started writing the memoir, I couldn't stop. I spent seven days a week in the computer room, being there for all three of the sessions it was open, morning, afternoon and reserve (evening). The more I wrote, the more memories came back to me. My entire life simply flowed out of me in written form. Shauna guided me and edited chapters as I wrote them, but she never told me what to write. She simply showed me how to write it. There was no pressure, only encouragement. It became the longest, most worthwhile project. I went through periods of not being able to stop writing, even handwriting at night in my cell. I also went through periods of not being able to write anything at all. Writer's block, I believe, is the term professional authors use. Despite this, writing was immensely therapeutic, and it brought me joy and pain in equal amounts.

I was so encouraged by my love of writing that I sought to do a degree in English Literature and Creative Writing with the Open University. I was approved, and it is something I am very proud of. Prison can be a very dark place, very draconian and demoralising. But the education facilities in all prisons are staffed by the most amazing people whose work goes unnoticed. The prison service needs to invest more in its education and to remove the roadblocks it has in place that hinder rather than help prisoners better themselves.

The days started to pass pretty quickly in Portlaoise. I developed a routine that I liked and became familiar with officers and fellow prisoners alike. I met people who were in for pretty heinous murders, transportation of vast quantities of drugs, terrorism offences, assaults and armed robberies. It was a veritable rogues' gallery. Somewhat worryingly, I fit in very well and found myself capable of holding conversations with them all, be they highbrow or pretty basic. There was always an undercurrent of fear in the place, but not of what you'd expect in a maximum-security prison. This fear was caused by the virus that was sweeping the world over: COVID-19.

It was approaching Christmas 2020, my first time not having Christmas dinner with the people that meant most to me. Visits to the prison were a disaster. There was a huge, thick Perspex screen separating you from your visitor. There was no hugging, kissing or contact of any kind. Conversation was difficult due to the fact that everyone had to wear masks, and it was impossible to hear through the thick screen. And the visiting room was always packed full of wives and small kids trying to communicate with their loved ones. I got a visit from my sister, and it was so disastrous, I simply told all friends and family thereafter not to bother. I couldn't hear a word she was saying to me as a result of the chaos. It was a total waste of her time. A three-hour round trip to spend 20 minutes trying to speak to each other through a thick Perspex partition and masks was bad enough, but couple that with the packed visiting room, and it was a disaster. I wonder if I was the only one who saw the irony of cramming maybe 90 people into the one visiting area during a pandemic, yet thinking they were managing the situation because there were Perspex partitions and masks.

It was shortly after this visit that prison started to get really depressing. COVID was rampant, and the Irish Prison Service, like many other organisations, simply had no idea how to manage it. The solution that the IPS came up with was to lock everything down. This meant putting all prisoners 'behind the door'. This simply meant we were locked in, 24 hours a day, 7 days a week. It was quarantine all over again, but worse. Your breakfast would be shoved in the door to you at 8 a.m., dinner at noon and tea at 4 p.m. I was subjected to two of these lockdowns, in January and December 2021. The January lockdown would prove to be a hugely significant period in my life, and it brought about huge change for me.

My days consisted of daytime TV, crime novels and more television. I don't think I was ever as clean in my entire life, because I was showering up to four times a day out of sheer boredom. You have no idea how important that shower in the cell was. I often thought of guys in the other prisons who had to go through lockdown getting out only twice a week for a five-minute communal shower in a filthy shower block.

It was about four days into lockdown. Yet another Groundhog Day was coming to an end. I wasn't feeling at all well but couldn't put my finger on why. I had no COVID symptoms, but I didn't feel right. I was having difficulty concentrating, and my eyes were going in and out of focus. I felt very panicky and nervous, and increasingly light-headed. I decided I'd have a shower and then climb into bed. But I never made it to the bed. I went into the shower, and the next thing I remember is me on the floor, looking up at three concerned officers, one of whom hit the panic button. A few minutes later, the doctor arrived. I drank plenty of water, and they helped me up on to the bed. The doc took my vitals and determined that I wasn't in need of a hospital visit. He told me that he had an idea of what was wrong but wanted to run a few more tests to be sure. He took blood and told me to stay in bed and drink plenty of water. Then he said that he'd see me in the morning.

The following morning came, and so did the doc. He was accompanied by a medic and an officer. I sat on the bed while he spoke to me through a crack in the door. He told me that the reason for my little episode was simple: I had type 2 diabetes, and my blood sugar levels were alarmingly high. I had long been warned by my doctor outside that I was a prime candidate for diabetes because of my ever-increasing waistline. I had always dismissed the possibility, telling myself that even if I did get it, it was nothing. Sure, millions of people live with diabetes every day. More delusion on my behalf. I liked the doctor. He was a down-to-earth Corkman, no bullshit, and he spoke to me like I was a human being, and not a piece of shit on the sole of his shoe like some prison staff did. He told me in no uncertain terms that my levels of diabetes were very concerning. He also told me that my weight and lifestyle were the main contributing factors. The tests he did revealed that if I was to continue living as I was, I wouldn't be living for much longer. He told me that, in his opinion, I would die in prison, given that I was going to be there for the next couple of years. Basically, he frightened the absolute shit out of me.

That day, I started on a course of diabetic medication. That was also the day that I started to cop myself on and take a seriously honest look at who I was, how I lived my life and what I wanted for my future. Not just from a health perspective, but also from a mental and a professional one. Life was about to take off.

I really threw myself into my schoolwork at this time. I was writing every day, under the tutelage of Shauna, the creative writing teacher. I was learning a lot and really enjoying it. One thing I noticed was that I was able to climb the stairs up to the school that much easier every day. The school was on the third floor, which involved 48 steps. I was doing this three times a day. I was sleeping better and felt more alert and positive. People were commenting on how well I looked, that I was losing a bit of weight, that the colour was returning to my cheeks. I always shrugged it off, but inside I was absolutely chuffed.

It was around this time that the chickens started coming home to roost, and the consequences of being in prison started to hit home. Other offences I had committed started to come to the attention of the gardaí. I got another six months added to my sentence for one of my more ridiculous schemes. In 2017, I'd heard of someone (who shall remain nameless) who needed a horsebox. I got word to him through another guy that I could source one, and next thing I knew, there was an envelope with €1,200 handed to me by an intermediary. Then I came up with a really dumb idea. I'd ring a few horse trainers, give them a big bullshit story about needing a horsebox on loan for a TV documentary I was making. I told them that I would of course return the horsebox, which had a market value of around €4k, when finished, presuming they'd either forget about it or I'd pay them back. After a few weeks, the trainer came looking for his horsebox. I had given it to he who cannot be named. The trainer started putting pressure on me to return the horsebox. The gardaí became involved, so I had to tell the guy I had sold it to. He didn't want the hassle and left it on the side of the street. The trainer came and collected it, and I repaid the guy I had sold it to. Problem solved. Problem solved, my arse! The trainer pursued his complaint, and I was charged with theft and deception. Six months consecutive. So, now I'm up to three and a half years.

The prison routine grew legs. I was walking more, going to the school more, and day by day I was becoming a part of the prison system. I was mixing on a daily basis with some of Ireland's most feared and hardened criminals, and in a strange, almost perverse, way, I wasn't intimidated by any of them. I was on first-name terms with Brian Rattigan, who ran the prison. Anything that needed to be done in C wing was only done with Brian's say-so. I had read and heard a lot about the guy. He had a reputation for violence, but he also had a working brain and the respect of the other prisoners. I never really had a lot to do with him, but the very fact that he'd always greet me with a big smile and a fist bump whenever we crossed paths earned me a certain amount of respect from other prisoners.

I was working in the library. One thing that the majority of prisoners love in a closed prison is watching box sets and DVDs on their Xboxes or PlayStations. I was in charge of the DVD collection in the jail, and I always made sure to notify the more influential prisoners and those I liked when the new releases were coming in. You never know in jail when you might need a favour, after all.

I had developed good relationships with most of the officers. I wasn't one of those prisoners who was always asking for things or demanding to see governors, and officers had a certain respect for that. There was a great contrast between the way I was treated compared to certain other prisoners. But then again, I was always polite, even when I didn't feel like it. I wasn't shouting at them, telling them that I knew where they lived, where their spouses and children lived. Being a frontline prison officer is a very fraught job. From what I have seen, alcoholism, drug addiction and gambling are all rife in a higher percentage of officers than people in other jobs. But there are several officers who deliberately go out of their way to antagonise certain prisoners; to be honest, if I had seen one or two of them getting a good slap, it would have brought a smile to my face. I saw this more in Limerick than anywhere else, but every prison I have been in on this journey had its bad apples in uniform.

Life in Portlaoise kept rolling along. To say it was like Groundhog Day would be a little harsh, because there was always a bit of drama floating around the place, but this time I was as regimented as I had ever been in my life. I had no problems at all, but that was about to change.

In May 2021, a detective from Kilrush, County Clare, asked to come and see me. I couldn't figure out what a cop from Kilrush would want from me, but he explained that the head office of An Post Money, the bank I had my account with, was based there. He then told me that he wanted to charge me with a scam I had pulled a year previously. It was a similar scam to the one that got me the sentence I was serving involving rugby tickets. This time, I was calling rugby clubs in England pretending to have Six Nations tickets. I got a guy who bit, and I proceeded to say yes every time he called me asking if I could get him extra tickets. I did this to the tune of €7,000, until the game was up. He started to get suspicious and wasn't long finding out all he needed to know about me. I hadn't been doing much in the way of covering my tracks. I had used my own name, address and phone number. Deep down, I always knew I was going to get caught, and I made it very easy for this guy to track me down. He gave me several opportunities to repay him or get him the tickets. Of course, I could do neither: the money had long since been gambled, and tickets were like gold dust by then. I left him with little or no option but to go to the guards, which he did. More charges coming. In fairness, the cop was true to his word. He told me that if I played ball he'd recommend that the charges be kept in the District Court, which he did. That didn't stop me from getting an extra nine months added to my ever-growing sentence. It now stood at four years and three months. And I wasn't finished yet.

CHAPTER 34

One of the best things about facing up to your demons while in prison is that you have an opportunity to 'clean house'. I knew I wasn't going anywhere for a while when I got locked up in October 2020, but I also knew that there was a world of other shit out there that was left behind when I went away. This 'shit' had come to haunt me pretty early into the sentence in the shape of the horsebox and rugby tickets incidents, but I knew there was more. I had thoughts about writing to the gardaí and admitting all. I didn't know whether the victims of other scams I had perpetrated had come forward and made complaints, but I figured that if I came forward, then I stood a good chance of getting credit for facing up to them if and when they went to court. As it stood, I was already serving sentences totalling four years and three months – surely to God, they couldn't lock me up for any longer, could they?

The opportunity was taken out of my hands almost as soon as I thought about it. One morning in Portlaoise the chief told me that a detective called Colm O'Sullivan wanted to talk to me, and he asked if I would do it voluntarily or wait to be arrested for it. Of course, I went the voluntary route, and I went down to the visits area to see him. O'Sullivan wanted to speak to me about a scam I had pulled in late 2019 with a company called DID Electrical. I think he was surprised at how candid and forthright I was with him. Our entire interview took 20 minutes. I caused him no problems, and he was happy to get it over with as much as I was.

Back in the day when I was working for Bob, one of the perks of the job was that companies would send in product samples for review in the hope of favourable publicity. Mobile phones were a prime example of this, and we'd regularly get the latest models. This was manna from heaven to someone like me. I'd grab the phones I wasn't going to use and take them to one of the many mobile phone shops in the Parnell Street area of Dublin, where I'd sell them for instant cash for half their market value. I got the cash and the guy in the shop got cheap phones – everyone's a winner.

However, when I was gambling like crazy and in desperate need of cash, this became a way for me to come up with an outlandish scam that would get me into a lot of trouble. I asked the guy who owned the phone shop what his buy rate for new iPhones was. He told me he was mad for stock and would give me up to €500 per phone. This drove me into a tizzy and sent me into a major tailspin. I came up with the idea that I would contact a major retailer and get stock on credit. I'd worry about how to repay it later. I rang DID and gave them a spiel about making a TV documentary, telling them that I'd need phones to set things up. I promised the company much-vaunted publicity for their assistance, and they bought into it immediately. I got four phones collected from their Fonthill Road depot by courier; I met the courier on Parnell Street, collected the phones and went to the phone shop. Fifteen minutes later, I was in the BoyleSports across the street with two grand burning a hole in my pocket. The two grand would be turned into ten, the bill to DID would be paid, and I'd still have a nice profit. Well, that was the theory. The reality was that I was on the train home an hour and a half later with barely enough money for a cup of coffee. I pulled this stroke with DID on two more occasions. When my account with them stood at €13,000 and no sign of it being paid, it was little wonder they got suspicious.

By then, the desperation was almost as insane as I was. All I could think of was gambling. I knew I was awaiting sentencing on the other charges, and I really didn't care about anything anymore. Life meant nothing to me at that stage. I absolutely detested myself, hating everything I was and had become. I hated the fact that I was a pitied, pathetic fuck-up; hated that I was morbidly obese; hated that I was going to jail; hated the fact that nothing gave me joy in life anymore – nothing. The occasional big win continued to give me false hope that the life-changing win was only around the corner.

I also pulled a similar stroke with an educational learning company and with Apple – both with identical results. I stole €9,000 worth of phones from the educational learning company and €2,500 from Apple. Both went to the gardaí. When I was later charged with the offence relating to the educational learning company while in Portlaoise, I requested a speedy hearing that would be uncontested. Judge Martin Nolan acknowledged that, despite my recidivism, he couldn't lock me up forever, and the 15-month sentence he gave me for all charges would run concurrent to my present sentence, meaning no extra jail time. I remember heading back to the prison van afterwards and the screws joking with me that I had done really well. I had, but I still felt sick. Nolan's words had a profound effect on me and served to regurgitate a lot of the self-hatred I had managed to deal with over the previous year and a half. The Apple matter was dealt with in Cork District Court by way of a 10-month sentence, similarly, to run concurrent to my present sentence.

*

In February 2022, I was transferred back to Limerick to see a doctor. My return to Limerick was everything I expected it to be, and more. I arrived around half past eight one night and was brought to D2 landing, the committal wing. The cell I was put in was filthy. I made the bed and didn't even bother turning on the telly. I went straight to sleep. Next morning, I had to meet the governor. I was then told I was going back to C2, the jungle. Back to square one.

Before I landed back in C2, I told the governor that my personal medical needs required privacy, and in fairness to him, I was given a cell to myself. Back in 2020, C2 had been a jungle. Now, in 2022, it made a jungle look like a holiday camp. I'd love to say that I took it all in my stride, that it didn't knock a stir out of me. I can't. The term in prison to describe a broken prisoner is 'smashed'. For my first few days in Limerick, I was smashed to fucking pieces. But I wasn't long getting my resolve back. It was then that I realised I really had changed as a person. I was no longer a yes man, a nodding dog that wanted to be loved and popular with everyone. And I liked the new me.

There was an assistant chief officer (ACO) in Limerick that I liked. I could count the number of officers in Limerick Prison that I could say that about on the fingers of one hand. Some of the remainder are bigger scumbags than any prisoner in the system. This ACO came to me shortly after I arrived, asked me how I was and told me that a few officers in Portlaoise that he knew were asking for me. He told me to keep my head down, my mouth shut and get on with things, and that I'd be transferred out in six weeks. He told me that Portlaoise was out of the question but he'd talk to a chief in Limerick that used to work in Wheatfield. According to him, the setup in the East Wing in Wheatfield was very similar to Portlaoise, with single cells with showers and a pretty good, enhanced regime. I couldn't fucking wait.

Two weeks into my Limerick sojourn, I got moved up to C4, which turned out to be a half-decent landing. I had a single cell, and there was a print workshop there where I got a job. The prisoners were mostly lifers or long-term prisoners, so there was considerably less drug use and fighting than there was down in the jungle. I was able to get to the school a couple of days a week, and I got to put in a few entries for the Writing in Prisons Award of Listowel Writers' Week. I was just beginning to get settled when I got word that I was to pack my bags. I was off to Wheatfield.

I arrived in Wheatfield on a Friday night. It was a huge complex, far bigger than Portlaoise or Limerick. I went through the regular routine at reception: my property got a quick examination by a few officers who, after a look at my file, knew that I wasn't going to give them any grief and that I wasn't stuffed like a turkey full of drugs. I was processed pretty quickly. I headed for 8F, the committal landing, not 30 yards and only one flight of stairs from 3G, a landing famous for being home to 'The Monk', Gerry Hutch, the man who didn't do the notorious Regency Hotel murder.

My landing was quiet, and it mostly housed guys for one night only before they were moved to a permanent landing. Of course, as was par for the course with me, there was a problem, and I had to spend two nights there before I was transferred to the East Wing. I went straight on to East 1 and immediately settled in. As the ACO in Limerick had promised me, it was very similar to Portlaoise: I had a spacious single cell with a shower; it was a big, bright landing; and it was far more relaxed than Limerick. There was a big library on the landing, and just one floor up was something I had long been thinking about reintroducing myself to: a gym.

The usual happened. Everyone on the landing converged upon my cell, all full of the same old questions: 'Where you from, bud?', 'Who do you know here?', 'What ya get fucked out of Portlaoise for?', 'Bring anything in with ya?' This time around, I was far more comfortable dealing with them, answering with nods and shoulder shrugs and acting aloof. I had survived almost two years in a hostile and volatile environment, and I coped fine. This place wasn't going to faze me.

The dynamics of each prison were very different. Limerick was raw, a powder keg that you expected to explode at any time. The officers were antagonistic and generally unpleasant. Portlaoise was more relaxed, yet it had a constant underlying current of potential violence of the highest level. The officers were generally more laid-back and respectful. Wheatfield was somewhere in-between.

I adapted well to life in Wheatfield. On my landing I got to meet some notorious characters. Jeffrey Dumbrell, part of an infamous family of brutally violent men, was serving his life sentence there, as was Brian Kearney, who killed his wife Siobhan in a grotesque act of violence many years ago. Brian was a diminutive character, kept himself to himself and spent his days learning Spanish. The most notorious fishes in the pond were Joe O'Reilly and a particularly vile individual named Brian Kenny, who was lifed off for the gangland murder of Jonathan O'Reilly in 2004. Joe O'Reilly strutted around the prison as if it was his own playground. He was loathed by everyone, officers and prisoners alike. Kenny was a different type of prisoner, more self-serving and snake-like.

I got a job in the computer and print workshop, working for an officer called Maxwell. Maxwell is definitely the best prison officer I've encountered. Nothing fazed him, there was no bullshit. He took you as he found you and expected you to do the same. He took no shit and dealt with any quickly when and if it arose. He appreciated the work done by us, and if he could do you a favour at any time, he would. He got me transferred to 5F, a 'super-enhanced' landing. It held only 16 cells and had its own communal living area, complete with leather sofas, washing machine, dryer, fridge, microwave and George Foreman grill. It also had a pool table and a 55-inch flatscreen TV on the wall. It was a 'cushy jail', as a prisoner would describe it.

I really started to expand my interest in writing here. I had an idea about publishing a magazine for the prisoners, something with content that prisoners would actually read, not the crap the IPS hands out, with rules and regulations all over it. This magazine had sports news, gangster profiles, what's on on Netflix and cash prize competitions. The governor, Miss Sutton, was fully supportive and encouraging. At first, I thought there might be a catch – my experience of governors up to this point was that they were all pen-pushing dinosaurs with no interest in prisoners rehabilitating themselves. I still hold this opinion, but Sutton was different. I saw her as ambitious and with a good grasp of how things needed to change in the prison system. I wouldn't be surprised to see her as the head of the IPS some day.

My time in Wheatfield went quickly. I spent a long, hot summer there. As prisons go, it would be best described as a happy medium. It had a lot of privileges and comforts, but it also had a seething undercurrent of potential violence and a bad drug problem. I didn't mind being there. It certainly beat the hell out of being in Limerick.

Towards the end of September, Maxwell called me into his office in the print shop. He told me that the governor had asked another prisoner to do the magazine going forward. I was really put out at this. I felt I had been doing a good job – the governor herself had told me as much – and I was just about to voice my concerns to him when he started smiling. He told me to calm down, that there was no problem, that this was a positive. It turned out that I was passed to go to Loughan House, and that the transfer was imminent. Maxwell couldn't tell me that at the time for security reasons, but that was something I really liked, even admired, about him. He was able to communicate well and get his point across.

That Saturday night, as we were banging in at seven, the class officer came to me and told me to be up early the next morning and start packing. I was off to Loughan. The final leg of my prison adventure was beginning.

CHAPTER 35

woke up the next morning around five, having been uneasy during the night. I was apprehensive – nervous, even. I couldn't explain it. This was all I had wanted for the past two years, and now that the time had come, I didn't know how I felt about it all. I had become quite settled in Wheatfield. I was on the super-enhanced landing, mostly with decent guys and good class officers. I loved working with Maxwell in the print shop. I had a nice cell with my own phone in it, and our own washing machine and kitchen facilities. Now, I was off to the big bad world of near-normal life, with semi-independent living. The truth is, I didn't know what to expect. I was full of fear and excitement.

At 8 a.m. we opened up the doors. I went around the other cells to tell the lads I was off. A guy from Cork that I was friendly with was also on the bus. I was happy for him. He was a good guy that got caught up in a toxic family situation that, coupled with alcohol, turned nasty. He ended up doing three years. At 9.30 we lugged our baggage down the drag, got put in a holding cell for half an hour, then loaded on to the infamous sweatbox, bound for the Cavan–Fermanagh border.

It was a horrendous journey. The fact that it took four hours on bad country roads was in itself a challenge. But if you add to that the fact that we were brought up by two 'strictly by the book' newbie screws who decided to slap the eights on us for the whole journey, you might understand why we were pissed off. You feel every bump in the road when shackled and confined to a cubicle even smaller than an airplane toilet.

We arrived in Loughan at around two. We went into the office of the ACO, a nice man who explained the basics and handed us our room keys and bedding kits. I was a bit pissed off to find out that I'd be sharing, but relieved to hear that whoever my new roomie was would be away until Wednesday night on his days home. The room was small, old and not at all what I had expected. But I had until Wednesday to come up with a plan. I went for a walk around the grounds. Loughan House can only be described as spectacular. It's set on 50 acres and overlooks Lough MacNean. The views out of my window were simply stunning. On my walk, I was approached by several different guys asking where I had come from and did I know so-and-so. I met a few guys I was in Portlaoise with. This helped me settle in. At 4 p.m. we grabbed tea in the canteen. Everyone ate together as a group. It suddenly dawned on me that this was the first time in two years that I had shared a meal with anyone. A scary thought.

That evening there was a football game taking place on the astro-turf pitch, so I strolled down to watch it. It was pretty competitive fare, between the Dubs and the Culchies. I crashed out about nine, and soon I was happily dreaming about something.

I woke at the crack of dawn next morning. As with all prisons, new committals have to meet the governor first thing the morning after they land. I went up to the office and joined a lengthy queue at Governor's Parade. I got to see him and had a good chat. He was a nice fella, dressed casually, a little gruff and rough around the edges. What I really liked about him was that he spoke to me like I was an equal, and not a prisoner. He looked at my file, told me that it was clear to him that I wasn't going to be a problem, and that I should be out of there in four to five months. This was music to my ears. After leaving his office, I went and met with the school principal. She was very friendly and helpful, too. She introduced me to the teacher who ran the computer room and gave me a timetable where I would have access all day, every day, should I want it. This was great and very helpful. In addition to completing my Open University work, I was able to write a large portion of this book there.

An open prison takes a bit of adjusting to. The freedom is hard to get accustomed to. I know that in the great scheme of things, I was only in a closed prison for two years, but you really do become institutionalised. I had gone from a strict regime of lockdown and constant supervision to a fully open-door regime that had little or no supervision, bar checking into the class office a few times in the evening to prove you were still there. It's little wonder many struggle to adapt. A lot of guys get sent back to closed prisons because they can't conform. There's too much easy access to drugs, plus the ability to just walk out the gate.

On the following Tuesday, I decided to use the diabetes card. There's an accommodation block in Loughan called Pine Lodge. It has all single rooms, it's bright and clean, and there's very minimal drug use there. Basically, it's inhabited by the prisoners who keep their noses clean and want to get out early. I went to the governor and told him that I was unhappy about having to share a room with anyone, since I was injecting myself with insulin. I pointed out the obvious problems that presented – needles, hygiene and so on – and I asked him for a room in Pine Lodge. There were a few empty rooms at the back they were keeping for COVID cases. He told me to go to the doctor and get confirmation that I would be taking injections. I got this done immediately, and next morning I was rehousing myself in Pine Lodge. Now I was really happy. Thank you, diabetes.

In an open prison you also have your own mobile phone. It's a basic Nokia that can only call and text, but it's a great bonus to be able to call as many people as you want, whenever you want. It's a huge perk, and I would now be able to talk to Mam as much as I wanted every day. It certainly helped to abate the constant worry I had around her.

In December I was approved for my weekends home programme. I was to get a three-night trial, and provided there were no problems, I would be entitled to one four-night period home each month until February and from then onwards two a month. Basically, I would be home every 11 days for a while. Finally, I could see some light at the end of a very long, dark tunnel.

Getting home was a real trek. My journey started at 7.38 a.m. with a bus from the gate of Loughan House to Sligo. Then I caught the 9.05 train to Dublin, which got to Connolly Station at 12.10. A quick hop on the Luas to Heuston and the 1 p.m. train to Limerick, getting in at 3.20 p.m. A seven-hour and 40-minute haul, but worth every bit of it. I jumped in a taxi and was home by 3.45. Then came the first shock.

Mam was at the door when I got home. It took her a few minutes to recognise me, as it did my sister. I suppose this was to be expected. They hadn't seen me in nearly two and a half years, and in that time, I had shed the equivalent of a normal person's body weight. I was literally half the man they had last seen. Then there was Mam's dementia. It had really taken its toll on her, and it was heartbreaking. But at least I was there. And I would be more regularly from then on. I didn't do much that weekend. I spent most of the time with Mam, chatting, catching up and telling her about life in 'Dublin' where

PAT SHEEDY

she thought I was working. I dropped in to see my mates. It hit me straightaway just how much these guys mean to me. There was no sentimentality, no questions – just plenty of the kind of banter that makes them the great bunch they are. It was as if I was never gone. I went back to Loughan on the Monday morning, a pre-7 a.m. start, arriving at 4.45 p.m. Long and tiring, but so so worth it.

Christmas came, and I got home again for a few days. I had missed the last three Christmas dinners at home. I was able to do a big shop and make a good old-fashioned Christmas dinner for Mam and me. It was great.

When I was gambling, I think I also had an addiction to clothes. I cleaned out the wardrobe and presses in my room and was absolutely appalled. Not only at the quantity of clothes (over 70 shirts and 40 pairs of jeans and chinos), but the sizes of them. My jeans had a 58/60-inch waist. My shirts were all XXXXXL. They looked like tents. I tried some on out of curiosity. It made me so proud of my achievements in losing the weight, but I was also disgusted that I had let myself go that badly. And all because of an addiction that had stripped me of every modicum of self-respect. I still haven't got rid of the clothes, but now that I'm home permanently I will. Hopefully, there are big guys out there that visit charity shops.

As I had done in the closed prisons, I engaged closely with the chaplain in Loughan House. Ita is an absolute angel sent from God. Like Joe in Portlaoise and Miriam and Glen in Wheatfield, she has dedicated her life to spreading the word to prisoners and being a constant crutch for them to lean on. I loved our chats, and I never missed a daily decade of the rosary with her. Chaplains really are a most undervalued part of prison staff, and definitely the most hard-working. I had been at home maybe two weeks when the postman delivered a big parcel to me one morning. I opened it to find a most beautiful framed holy picture from Ita by way of thanks for helping her with a few things while I was there, along with the loveliest letter. Ita and Joe are going to be in my daily thoughts for a very long time.

In April I received a nice phone call from Tom Shortt, the arts and education officer in the Irish Prison Service. He notified me that I had been successful with my entry to the Listowel Writers' Week 2023, and that since I was on a temporary release programme, I would be invited to the awards night at the festival in May. I would be the first prisoner to accept an award in person in the 42-year history of the festival. I was given three extra days temporary release from the governor to attend the ceremony. I travelled to Listowel with Tom and was blown away by the reception I received from a rather large crowd when I went up to accept the award. I spoke honestly about my life and my struggles. It was a hugely emotional five minutes. I was walking back to my seat, when I noticed the renowned actor Stephen Rea leading a standing ovation for me that seemed to last forever. I wanted the floor to open up and swallow me. I didn't know where to look and really felt out of place. I felt I didn't belong in an audience like this. But after the event, quite literally everyone in the crowd came and shook my hand. People like Stephen Rea, Marie Heaney (wife of the late literary legend Seamus) and BBC journalist Manveen Rana all spoke to me, offering words of encouragement. I left Listowel that night with a swelled head and a new-found confidence that maybe, just maybe, I do have a story to tell, one that people will want to hear. And that some will *need* to hear.

I really wanted to be home right then. It was getting harder and harder to return to Loughan House after my time home. I was practically at home as much as I was in prison at this stage, and I had started to get very accustomed to living a normal life again. But, prison being prison, it was always on my mind that I had to go back. I was still a prisoner and the Irish Prison Service basically owned me until my release date. I had started to apply some pressure to the governors and to the Probation Service to try and secure a community return programme in order for me to be at home permanently. I noticed more and more that Mam needed somebody at home on a full-time basis at this stage, as the dementia continued to take from her quality of life. I still felt hugely guilty, not for the dementia, but for the fact that I had left her to fend for herself while battling such a disgusting disease. It also rankled me that other people in the prison were getting released with a lot longer left on their sentences than I had. But there was a reason for that, and because I wasn't the type of criminal with knowledge of the drug and gangland worlds to impart, I simply didn't fit into that category.

In mid-July, I started to see progress. Probation called me for interviews and meetings. Soon after, I was approved for a community return scheme, a programme that entails three mornings a week working to benefit the community. It's practically identical to the community service that I did back in the 1990s. I was released on 9 August and, now that I have finished my 14-week stint of community return work, my sentence is officially finished. It was a surreal experience, walking out that gate for the final time. Being back home permanently took a bit of getting used to. Three years had passed – at times, in the blink of an eye, at other times, in what felt like a lifetime.

Looking back, I can best sum up how I feel about my prison experience by using an entry to a writing competition that was run by the librarian in Loughan House. To enter you had to write a story in six words. That's not as easy as it sounds, and some of the entries were really good. I wasn't allowed to enter because I had won the Listowel festival, and nobody would enter if they thought I was going to. The entry that won, and that stuck with me, was:

Was it worth it? ... Probably not.

ACKNOWLEDGEMENTS

This book wouldn't have been possible without the support and encouragement that I received throughout. Top of that list is Shauna Gilligan, a great writer, brilliant teacher and even better person. Shauna gave me not only the knowledge of how to write, but also the confidence in myself to do it. Writing this book got me through some very dark times and gave me a daily purpose while in prison, and it wouldn't have been written without Shauna. Honourable mentions go to Dave Higgins, Evelyn Dunne, Anita Dooley, Brenda McCormack, Angela Dennehy, Sinead McCabe and Caitriona Kelly.

I've mentioned the prison chaplains in this memoir, so the debt of gratitude I owe each of them is obvious. To Joe, Miriam, Glen and Ita: may God continue to bless you all. Please don't ever stop doing what you do.

To Patricia Hogan, for all the help and encouragement she gave me, for giving me an unknown number of kicks in the arse when I needed them and for being a great counsellor. The same applies to my prison counsellors Noeleen and Ann-Marie. The work done by these fantastic women is hugely underappreciated and under-resourced.

The encouragement shown to me by Tom Shortt, the arts and education officer at the Irish Prison Service, has been and still is phenomenal. He has opened doors for me that I could never have opened, and his passion, pragmatism and sagacity shine through in his personality. Education in prison is a potential lifeline for all prisoners and a great opportunity for rehabilitation. Sadly, the powers that be that run our prison service don't seem to see it like that. Rather than support and encourage prisoners to attend school in our closed prisons, they have placed unnecessary roadblocks in the way that can discourage and prevent prisoners from grasping the life-changing nettle that I was able to grasp. The educators that work in our prisons are amazingly gifted. Society would surely be a better place if they were allowed more time and resources to improve the lives and minds of prisoners who both want and need improvement.

Finally, to those that matter the most to me – my family and friends. I've let you all down more times than I can recount. I've broken more promises and caused you all a world of pain and shame that none of you deserve. You have all fought my corner when that corner was an impossible place to defend. All I can do is not put you through any more of that. I love you all and am sorry.

Thank you.